LIFE WITHOUT MUM

2011

Published and Printed by

Leiston Press
Masterlord Industrial Estate
Leiston
Suffolk
IP16 4JD
01728 833003
www.leistonpress.com

ISBN - 978-1-907938-15-3

This is my book of my own personal experiences of my life
without mum.
My life has been a very long journey since 1989
When sadly my mum past away of breast cancer
At the age 39, married with 7 children
My youngest brother was only 18months old.
When my mum past away her wish was for me to take care of my
3 younger siblings
When i was told mum was dying my world as i knew it was the start
of my life changing forever.
My mum and me had the most unique bond a mother and daughter
could ever have that not even death could take away
The death of my mum and her wish she left behind to me is where my
long and endless journey all begins.

WRITTEN BY MRS SHARON MASON

On Friday the 31st March 1989 at ten past eight was the worst day of life and would change my life forever. Mum was my world and without mum in it, my life as i knew it was no more, i felt i had no life to live, I felt lost and distraught as a person, i was only 16 years old when my mum past away and didn't know such pain ever existed, i knew when mum died a big part of me died to and that part could never be replaced. All i knew was my heart was with my mum and i no longer wanted to live my life without her in it. But i had to live and that reason was my mum's wish for me to take care of my younger siblings and that was the only reason i had for living. The hardest part was losing mum, the second hardest part was going from a 16 year old girl to being like a replacement mother to my own brothers and sister. I felt my life at that point so hard to carry out mums wish and greave for her at the sametime. I tried to carry on where my mum had left off and for me that was the hardest part to bair. To be in our home where mum used to be, but yet no longer was. I was doing all the things she would do. After my mum's death my dad took two weeks off of work so we could all be together as a family to cope with the loss of mum. At times i felt i could not cope and at other times i knew i had to push myself to do so. A few months after mum past away life for me was still so raw and everyday that past life was still full of pain, it felt like a bad dream and that one day i would awaken from this terrible nightmare and mum would still be alive, but this was no dream, this was my life and it was real. Just when i felt i was doing my mum proud my dad dropped a bomb shell on me and said he had met another Woman. Just when i didn't think my world could get any more unbearable it just did. I couldn't bair to see my dad with someone else so soon after losing mum, i hated myself. I had tried so hard to be everything mum use to be, i thought me and my younger Siblings would be enough for my dad, but we wasn't. We couldn't give to my dad what he felt he needed to start rebuilding his life again, and because i couldn't accept what my dad wanted he asked me to leave the family home. As hard as it was for me to leave our family home knowing that i failed my chances of carrying out my mum's wish it felt like i was abandoning my younger siblings to, I knew In my own heart i had to leave for my own sanity if nothing else, my mind at this point felt like it was going to explode.

How could this all be happening to me, my life was falling apart quicker than i knew how to put it back together again. When my mum was alive i had a boyfriend, mum never did like him she always said he was trouble, but being young you only see what you want to see. I was seeing him on and off throughout the time i was looking after my younger siblings, so with no place to go i went and stayed with him at his parent's house. The first night i cried myself to sleep i missed my mum so much and now being away from my siblings i just didn't see any reason for living anymore, the pain i felt was gut wrenching. I felt so alone in this big wide world, i never knew how you could have it all One minute and in a blink of an eye it's almost as if someone has opened a window and a gust of wind has blown through and taken your life away. I stayed for a while at my boyfriend's house, and then i went into a homeless unit. It was up Anglesea road Ipswich, it was a tiny room no bigger than a small bathroom of a 3 bedroom house. What was more unbearable is where the room i was in was situated. It was situated dead opposite the hospital where my mum had died. My boyfriend didn't want to stay with me, so once he had left and the door was shut i was all alone. I had so many mixed emotions running through my head, when i looked out of my window i would have flash backs of when mum died. I felt like i had had my heart ripped out again. Within a matter of hours i knew i couldn't go on anymore, i had lost my only reason for living.I wanted my life Now to be with my mum, so with no one there to stand in my way i decided to take an overdose, it was my only way of escaping the terrible aching pain i could no longer control. I waited and slowly drifted off to sleep hoping i would soon be back with my mum only to be woken up by a paramedic. I was taken to hospital to have my stomach pumped. When i finally Came around i saw my best mate sitting by my bedside crying, we just hugged each other, She saved my life but at that moment in time it wasn't what i wanted but i guess it just wasn't my time. My dad came up to see me, he was angry for what i had done to myself. He was upset so we hugged and he told me never to do it again. The next day i was discharged from hospital and within a few days i was moved in to another homeless unit but this time my boyfriend stayed with me.

Little did i know as time went by i found myself in an abusive relationship. Where did it all come from, i still ask myself the same question to this day. A few more months went by and one month i didn't come on my period so i did a pregnancy test and it came back that i was pregnant, finally i had a reason for living again someone for me to love, I phoned my dad to tell him that i was having a baby, but my dad was not happy, for me though it was the light at the end of the tunnel. Dad got me my own flat on the condition i didn't see my boyfriend anymore, so i agreed and moved into the flat on my own, I felt so alone again thinking of my old life, missing my mum, my two brothers and sister. As time went by i started seeing my boyfriend again behind my dad's back. The months went by and he started being abusive again, so i found myself in the same abusive relationship throughout my pregnancy. Then suddenly i went into labour a month early, i had my boyfriend with me and his mum but all i wanted was my mum. I was crying a lot throughout my delivery and finally after hours of pain, tears, and pushing i had a baby girl weighing 6lbs 2oz and she was perfect in every way. When i held her in my arms for the first time i said to myself that night i took my overdose wasn't my time and this was the reason why my beautiful baby girl ,i named her after my mum. What i would of gave to have had my mum here with me nobody will ever know. There is no one like your mum and every girl needs their mum. My mum from the day i lost her will always live on inside my heart. When i go to her grave side where she was buried nobody will ever know the pain i feel as i turn around and leave her there only i know that. When my boyfriend left the hospital and went home, being alone with my daughter holding her in my arms looking down at this tiny person i knew she depended on me to love her, protect her to the best of my ability, and to be the best mum that i could possibly be for her. I wanted my little girl to look up to me throughout her life. I wanted her to grow up to be as proud of me as her mum, as i was of mine. I was in hospital for seven days, then me and my daughter went home, not a day went by that mum wasn't on my mind. After the birth of our daughter my relationship with my partner went from bad to worse, his drug habit got worse, and he started to get into crime, he spent more time away from me and our daughter than he did being at home with us. It wasn't long before i found myself in a situation where i didn't know what to do for the best. He started spending the rent money for our flat and before i knew it i ended up being evicted and back in another homeless unit down London road. I was slowly slipping into depression, i also got tangled up on the wrong side of the law by him just teaching me how to drive, we ended up getting into a police chase with our daughter in the back seat of the car, when the chase came to a standstill, my boyfriend jumped out of the car and done a runner from the police and left me there alone to deal with the police. After being taken to one side while my daughter was left crying in her car seat, i was told by a very understanding policeman why they were after my boyfriend, he told me on the sly that if i didn't walk away from him i stood a good chance of losing my little girl to social services if i carried on seeing him, I was told no charges would be brought upon me and was driven home by the policeman. After being dropped off i walked into my room and my mind was made up i was never going to let any harm come to my daughter and therefore ended our relationship. My little girl at this time was only 6months old and she had to be my number one priority. I was still deeply in love with my boyfriend as he was all i had left apart from my daughter. I had not seen my dad or my younger siblings for a long time as my dad had got me my flat on the understanding i wouldn't see my boyfriend anymore, so choosing to be with him i had lost my flat, my own self respect but the bottom line was my head was one big mess as i had already lost so much. Mine and my dad's relationship was up and down all the time. In that period of time i didn't get to see my younger siblings and that broke my heart, because while i was not seeing them i felt as if i was failing my mum as she had asked me to take care of them. My boyfriend was very controlling throughout our relationship and me ending our relationship he was not going to let that go, we ended up seeing each other again. A few weeks down the line in the early hours of the morning i heard a very loud knock on the door with the police shouting through the door open up it's the police. My boyfriend shouted at me not to open the door, but i went against what he asked me not to do and i opened the door, 3 policemen rushed in, grabbed hold of him and then put him in a set of hand cuffs and read him his rights, they then took him away. My little girl was crying as they took my boyfriend away to the police car. I just shut my door and picked up my little girl, she was so upset. I never wanted my daughter to get hurt and i would do everything in my power to stop her from ever getting hurt again. The next day my boyfriend was in court and was sentenced to 3 years in prison and to me it was a god send, because i knew he could no longer hurt me or my daughter again whilst he was in prison. I found it hard to adjust at first as being with my boyfriend every day was different, i never knew what was going to happen next in my life but after time i adjusted to life without him. Then one day my dad pulled up outside my homeless unit and told me he had someone in the car who wanted to see me, so i walked out and in the back seat of the car was my 3 younger siblings and right away i could not hold back my tears, i was so over whelmed with joy to see them, my heart skipped a beat, my dad then asked me if i wanted them for the weekend and it was a dream come true for me. We had all missed each other so much i had the best weekend ever just being with them for two whole days. Words couldn't explain how good it felt to have them back in my life again. Dad picked them up on the Sunday night and told me i could have them again the following weekend, so i said goodbye to them and told them how much i loved them. It was so hard to let them go again but i was just looking forward to the following weekend when i could be with them again. After mum died it meant so much to me spending all that time with them at the family home everyday i got closer and closer to them. I stopped looking at them as my brothers and sister and looked at them as my own children, i did everything for them that a mother would do cooking, cleaning, taking them to school putting them to bed with dad being at work. Taking care of them was all i had. My brother was 6 when mum past away and i will never forget when i was at the family home taking care of them, my brother said out of the blue can we catch a bus to heaven so we can go and see mummy it broke my heart, so i took him outside and i told him to look up at the sky and when you see the brightest star at night you know that's mummy and she's looking down on you because she wants you to know she is still with you, watching over you and most of all she will always love you. It wasn't long before the following weekend was here and i had my brothers and sister again, once more being with them felt so good, it made me think of mum so much more when i was with them because us kids were mum's world. Knowing how young they were and how much they all still needed her and that they would never grow up knowing who mum was or having any real memories of her broke my heart. So seeing my younger siblings meant the world to me but heart breaking memories came with it to. I loved taking them to the park and watching them play, to see them smile and laughing away with my daughter and just being able to spend time with them at weekends. Later on in the school holidays i had them as often as i could and slowly i started to feel i was doing what mum ask me to do and i felt at peace with that. Whenever i had them i would always talk to them about mum letting them know how much of a special person she was hoping that as they grew they would have some memories of mum they could treasure. As the months went by i started seeing my younger siblings more and more, they started to become a very big part of my life again. My boyfriend was writing me letters whilst he was in prison and one day i received a letter from him saying he was coming out on day release. I didn't know how i felt about the thought of him being out as i was still in love with him even after all he had put me through. Just when i had started to try and make a life for myself him coming out made life complicated for me again, it stirred up all mixed emotions about how i really felt for him but at the same time did i want to let him back into my life again after all he had put me through. Before i knew it the day of his day release was here and i let him come back home, when i saw him after such a long time i knew i was still very much in love with him. We had a really nice day with our daughter and it felt like he had changed, we ended up making love. It was too good to be true, he had made a fool of me again as he had to be back at the train station for five o' clock but decided to tell me that he wasn't going back to prison and my troubles started all over , my head was a mess once again. It was the worst move i could have ever made letting him back into my life. He got very controlling and abusive. I had kidded myself thinking that he had changed. He decided he was going to go on the run which in total he was on the run for a month. In that time i knew no matter what while he was out of prison even if i wanted to i didn't stand a chance of getting way from him until he was caught by the police, he was laying in the bath one morning and i said to him as soon as you go back to prison I'm leaving you for good this time as i don't want this life anymore, he just laughed at me and said who's going to want you with a kid then. He then turned round and said you will never leave me so i just turned around and walked away. I wanted so bad to ring the police and tell them where he was but it was more than my life was worth, so i just hoped and prayed it wouldn't be long before he was caught. After a few weeks my dream had come true he had been picked up by the police and sent back to prison to do the rest of his sentence with an extra 28 days on top for going on the run. I was so relieved that he was back in prison, but i had let more damage be done to me and my daughter, i hated myself for that and i should of known better. I was determined that this time it was over for good, being with someone that was so controlling and abusive was not that easy to break away from, Me and my daughter started to get back to life the best we could after her dad was taken back to prison. One day i woke up and felt really unwell i hadn't come on my period that month so i done a pregnancy test and it showed i was pregnant again, i couldn't believe what i saw i just sat there in a daze stairing at the test showing that i was pregnant, my life was in such a mess. Mentally i couldn't cope with life as it was, but i have never believed in having abortions so i decided i was going to go ahead with my pregnancy. I booked a visit to the prison to go see my daughter's dad to tell him i was pregnant. He was so happy saying i will change when i get out we will be a proper family. It didn't make any difference to me what he was saying as i knew in my own mind our relationship was over and whilst he was in prison he couldn't get to me so i left and made my way home. I was still seeing my younger siblings throughout my pregnancy but my life was getting harder as i was still in the homeless unit. I had a good size room with my own kitchen, it was just big enough for me and my daughter but with the new baby coming along and when my younger siblings stayed at weekends it just wasn't suitable for us anymore, so me and my friend who was in the unit with me decided we would get a flat together as she had a daughter the same age as my daughter. Months went by and i had a very stressful pregnancy, one night i woke up in a lot of pain and ended up going into hospital and gave birth to a baby boy weighing 4lb s 2oz, he was born 6 weeks early and had to stay in hospital for three weeks as he was so tiny. They had to build him up before he was allowed to come home. My dad came up to see my son and fell in love with him as soon as he saw him, dad came to pick me up as i was discharged from hospital the next day but i felt so sad leaving the hospital as my son was not coming home with us, me and my daughter went up the hospital everyday to see my son. My younger siblings when i had them use to come up to and it wasn't long before my son was aloud home for the first time. My daughter was so good with him as she had to adjust from it only being me and her, she loved her brother to bits and my two brothers and sister loved coming over to spend time with my two children. I missed my mum so much no matter what i had in my life even after having two children of my own and seeing my younger siblings there was always a big empty space in my heart with mum not being here anymore. From the day mum died once a week to this day i always go up to her grave side to sit and talk to her, my daughter as soon as we were near my mum's stone would run along and kiss the picture of her that was on her stone. It was hard but i talked all the time to my daughter about her nanny, what she was like and that she would of loved to have been here playing with her. The way i saw it even though mum was not with me anymore i wanted my children to grow up knowing what a great person mum was and that someone who is not with us anymore can still be respected for the person they were. Having memories of mum is what keeps her alive in my heart and in my children's heart's for years to come. I was still receiving prison letters from my children's father but i had stopped sending letters in reply because i knew the relationship was over now for me and i just wanted to put the whole relationship behind me. I met my boyfriend when i was 14 years old and our relationship lasted 7 years on and off. Being with him the way he was changed me as a person with him being in and out of prison, all the drug taking, being in an abusive relationship. I owed my children a better quality of life than that. The only good thing that came out of mine and his relationship were my two beautiful children and without our relationship i wouldn't have conceived them and i wouldn't change that for anything. A few months went by and still the letters kept coming, so i decided to go and visit my ex partner in prison to tell him straight the relationship was over, so me and my daughter went up while my mate looked after my son at home. My daughter stayed in the play centre at the prison while i saw her dad, I ask him to stop sending me letters because the relationship between us was over. He started to cry and begged me not to leave him but i wasn't falling for any of it this time and said i am sorry but there was nothing else left for us to say, i told him just to look after himself and then left the visiting room. I picked my daughter up from the play centre and made our way back to the train station, I didn't feel anything for their dad anymore i loved him as the father of my kids but i was no longer in love with him. I was happy for it just to be me and my two children, he never knew his son and he only knew our daughter until she was 6 months old before he went on the run, but he didn't spend any time with her, i wanted so much more for them than that and i was happy with the decision i had made because my children would always come first. Me and my daughter got on to the train and half way home my little girl started playing with this man sitting in front of our seat, she kept hitting him on the head with her hand and ducking down when he turned round to look at her, she found that so funny she just wouldn't leave him alone, i kept trying to look at what he looked like in the window as she kept on playing with him, then i ask her to stop so she did. I took my daughter to the toilet and on our way back to our seats my little girl smiled at him and he smiled back, for some reason after only just ending my relationship with their dad knowing i wasn't looking for another relationship this feeling i got in my tummy i had never felt before. Suddenly the train had stopped and it was time to get off the train, I stood up with my little girl and then so did the man in front, he turned and looked at me and said i love her trainers she's so sweet. Walking away after getting off the train me and my daughter stood at a set of traffic lights and blow me away the same man walked up behind us and said hi again we have got to stop meeting like this, i replied i know, where are you from i asked him. He replied i originally come from Peterborough but i am staying at light foot house, i replied oh ok the lights then changed. He said goodbye then walked one way and i walked the other and that was the last we saw of him. On my way home i couldn't shake of this weird feeling i had in my tummy there was just something about him, me and my daughter finally got home and i told my mate all what had happened at the prison and i said what i had to say to their dad and left it at that. I then said to her something really weird just happened on the train on the way back. So i explained to her how my daughter was playing with this man who sat in front of us, she kept hitting him over the head and ever since i had got off of the train and saw him again at the traffic lights i have had this weird feeling in my tummy and that i really liked him, my mate asked me if i had got his number and i said no he comes from Peterborough, so i won't see him again. I spent all night talking about this man i saw on the train, i just couldn't get him off my mind, a few days went past and me, my mate and our children had to go down to the social to get our weekly money, we sat on the floor waiting to be called in. Our two girls were out playing near the stairs of the of the social when suddenly my daughter came running in towards me nearly falling over saying mummy that's that man, at first i didn't realise who she was talking about. Then as i looked up i saw him my tummy started going weird again i looked up at him and he said hi again, i had butterfly's in my tummy, i didn't know why i was getting these feelings as i had never felt like this before not even when i had first met the father of my kids.

He sat on a seat with his mate, i kept looking at him and he kept looking at me, then he was finally called in. When they called him in i managed to catch his name, so at least now i knew his name, minutes later my mate and me were called in and when we walked through the door there he stood, my heart started racing, butterfly's going mad in my tummy. What was going on i asked myself in my own head what is it with this man, he then walked past me smiled and said goodbye. We left the social and i said to my mate that's the man on the train that i told you about, my mate couldn't believe it she said why didn't you get his number, i replied to her i don't know. I couldn't come to grips with the way i felt when i saw him i knew i was not ready for another relationship, i had been through so much already but there was something about him that i just couldn't explain. We got back home to our flat and i was driving my mate mad just going on and on about him. This lasted till late that night, then i remembered him saying he was staying at light foot house so i told my mate, she replied you know where light foot house is don't you and i said no. She replied it's only down the road from us, i said no way your joking, she said no i'm not. With that i begged and begged her if she would go to light foot house I had the biggest ache in my heart i had fallen hard for this man, so i wrote a note with our address asking him to come round at one o' clock and asked my mate would she post it for me, she said no i 'm not but with a bit more persuading she finally said yes if you shut up and go to sleep. I couldn't sleep all night long. I just couldn't get him out of my head. Morning came and my mate dropped the note off and i waited patiently for one o' clock to arrive, suddenly there was a knock at the door, my mate went to the door and he came walking through our living room and said hi, I said hi back, we all sat chatting for a few hours and Stephen and his mate said they had to go somewhere but that they would be back in an hour, once he had left i said to my mate i don't know if i like him now we have started speaking. My mate replied why he's really nice, let them come back and see how you feel when they get back, I think it was all going too fast for me as i had only just ended my relationship with my children's dad and i found it really hard to trust a another man after being with him. There was a knock on the door he came walking through and we all started talking again. The night came to an end i walked him towards my front door to see him out and he asked me do i get a goodnight kiss then, so we had a little kiss and he said can i see you again tomorrow and i replied yes i would like that. After he left me and my mate sat talking for a few hours about how i felt about him as earlier on in the night i commented that i didn't know if i liked him. I said there is something about him and i can't wait to see him again tomorrow, i 'm just scared because i have so much going on right now in my life but there is just something about him and i have never felt this way before. The next day soon arrived and i saw him again, he loved my little girl they took to each other straight away. I was still getting letters from my children's dad so i decided to go up one last time to visit him again the next day. So me and my daughter went up to the prison again to see him, i had left my little boy at home with my mate and once we arrived at the prison i left my daughter in the play centre again. I ask him once again to stop writing me letters because we were over, with that he replied you've got someone else haven't you, i replied it's not that i just don't want to be with you anymore. He got angry and said if i am with anyone he had better know how to take care of himself so i ended our conversation and walked away. I went to get my daughter and we left the prison, when we finally arrived home i walked through the door and Stephen was there waiting for me holding my son in his arms, i shook all over as i never told him i had another child. It was such early days of seeing him i felt it was too early to introduce him to my son, he already knew i had a little girl but i also remembered the comment my ex had made the time he laid in the bath, that who would want me with a kid, i had already started to like him and my daughter being two at this point had really taken to him, to my amazement Stephen just said to me i didn't know you had a son he is gorgeous, what a sigh of relief that was to hear,i replied to him i didn't know how you would feel about me having two children. Stephen just replied i love kids, i had also told him on the first night we had met that i still had a picture on my wall of me and my kids dad. Stephen asked where i had been today, I lied and said to see my brother in prison i couldn't bare to tell him it was the father of my kids because i had really fallen for him at this point. I had only just ended my relationship with my ex so soon after i saw him for the first time on the train and i didn't want to start a relationship with Stephen if we were going to be together based on lies, so i ask him to come to my room and told him i had to tell him something. He replied i all ready knew it wasn't your brother i knew it was your boyfriend. I said no he's not my boyfriend he's the father of my two kids and he got sent to prison for three years and I'm not with him anymore. I explained i had to go to the prison again as the first time i went i told him we were over and to stop sending me letters but the letters still kept coming, so i went today to ask him once again to stop sending the letters because the relationship between us was over. He just won't let me get on with my life, Stephen was so understanding even though i didn't tell him the truth he total understood, we spent a long time talking and it felt like a load had been lifted. I told him all about my mum and my younger siblings as i had them staying with me that weekend, i also asked Stephen why he was at light foot house he told me it was because he had pinned up a security guard and that he had to answer bail in a week's time, i kept asking myself is this relationship going to be any different to the relationship i had with my children's father, but somehow i don't know why but i knew he was the one for me. We had been seeing each other for two weeks now and we all enjoyed every minute of it. My mate had fallen in love with one of Stephen's mates and she decided to move out and get her own flat. After only two weeks of seeing each other me and Stephen were so in love, i know it sounds mad but we had fallen head over heels for each other and my children loved him to bits. He was so good with them and i was so shocked at that because knowing that they were not his children by blood. My younger siblings even took to him and when we were all together it felt like i had been with him forever. We sat and talked one night as the next day he had to go to court as he was out on bail until his sentencing. I said to Stephen i wish that you could stay and live with us as we miss you when you have to go home, he replied i can stay with you and the kids all i have to do is change my bail address to yours and that was what we did. We had only been together two weeks and we were already living with one another and it was great. I was not a hundred percent sure that i was doing the right thing as i just didn't want me and my children to get hurt again. It just felt so right though, there had to be a reason for us getting together after the way we met. We were talking one night and telling each other how we felt the first time we saw each other on the train, he said he couldn't stop talking about me all night saying he wished he would of asked for my number. He had told his mates he saw a gorgeous girl on the train and she had a daughter that was so sweet and he thought that he would never see me again, the day we had seen each other down the social he had said to his mate wouldn't it be nice if that girl was here.

That's when he walked through the doors and looked up the stairs, he said to his mate she's here and his mate replied how do you know and Stephen said because that's her daughter, if she's here her mum is, He also told his mate i'm going to have that girl, his mate replied no way you will never get her and Stephen said i will. So little did we both know we were talking and thinking about each other at the same time, Even though i had fallen in love with him, not a day went by that i didn't think about my mum, So much had gone on in my life in such a short space of time it felt like i was on a roller coaster and i just wanted it to slow down so that i could get a grip on what was going on in my life, everything was moving so fast for me. The week finally arrived for Stephen to go back to court, i asked my mate to look after my two children as we had to go back to Peterborough court. We got on the train and being back on the train together after only knowing him for less than a month felt really weird as that was where we both saw each other for the first time. We both felt nervous not knowing what was going to happen in court, but one thing we both knew for sure was that we both wanted to be together. The train took two and a half hours to get to Peterborough and we were holding hands all the way there, it's like we just didn't want to let go of each other. Before Stephen had walked into our lives, life for me was unbearable after mum's death but with him being around made my life a little more bearable .We got off the train and made our way towards the court, i had really bad butterfly's, Stephen did to. We sat waiting till they called out Stephen's name, i was shaking all over Stephen stood in the dock and i sat in a row of seats in the front line of the court room, a lot was said to Stephen by the judge and then finally the judge asked Stephen to stand and said i sentence you to five months in prison and the hammer went down. The two policemen were told to take Stephen down to the cell's, i couldn't believe what was happening i went to the bathroom of the courts and then waited to see if i could see Stephen before they took him to prison, i was so upset. Why i kept asking myself, cant for once in my life something go right for me. After a while i got called in by a policeman to go and see Stephen, i sat down and we were both crying Stephen was shocked he said to get five months when his solicitor had told him he was looking at community service or probation at the worst, it was so hard i just didn't want to let him go. How could i hate him for what he did, when he had got into trouble with the law before we had even met, Stephen kept asking will you wait for me i love you and the kids so much, i know it's a lot to ask you to do after all you have gone through, but i don't ever want to lose you, with tears rolling down both our faces i said hugging him of course i will wait for you i love you so much. I just don't want to let you go he said i will write to you everyday, i replied i will to and he said when you get back home give the kids a big kiss for me and tell them i love them and that i will be home soon. Then the policeman came in and said times up so we hugged and we had the longest kiss, i wanted it to last forever. With tears running down our faces i didn't want to let go of him, then the policeman said come on then Stephen time to go, as he started to walk towards the policeman with us still holding hands, slowly our hands were just slipping away from each other, i watched him walk away still in tears saying i love you babe, i said crying i love you to always. Then he was gone, i started to make my way out of the court and i felt so alone again. All the way to the train station i just couldn't get it together i had finally met the man of my dreams and after only a month i had lost him. My train pulled up and i got on the train sitting in the same seat's we had both sat in on our way to the court. Just looking by the side of me at the empty chair that he had sat in on the way here, tears still rolling down my face, my heart was in bits. Five months doesn't seem long but at that point it felt like a life sentence for us both. I couldn't stop thinking about him as this was the first time he had been to prison, we were both so happy for such a short time that we had spent together and we were so in love. People sometime's say they don't believe in love at first sight but from the first time we set eyes on each other On that train we both knew there was a connection between us that not even words could explain. It was like we were chosen to be with each other. That's like his birthday was on the day my mum died on the 31st of March and on the day of mum's birthday i would be in bits as when she was alive i had always brought her something for her birthday no matter how big or small the present was it always lit up her eyes. From the day mum died it was a very painful day for me to get through. I could no longer buy her gifts anymore. The most i could buy my mum now was her favourite bunch of flowers that she loved. There was no seeing that light in my mum's eyes like i use to see anymore. I do believe in life after death as i have always felt my mum's presence around me, not everyone believes in that but i think when we lose a loved one, sometimes we will always feel them around us in some part of our life and i do believe that me and Stephen were meant to be together. Maybe that's why Stephen's birthday was on the day that mum died, that was her way of replacing a sad day for me. For a day that was replaced with a happy day and not such a painful day for me to bair. I was in tears on and off all the way home thinking what to tell my children when they asked me where Stephen had gone and just running through my head how i was going to get through the next two and a half months but i told myself as long as i had my children and my younger siblings in my life i will get thought this. I finally made it home as time was getting on and when i walked through my front door my mate jumped up out of her chair and said i was so worried where have you been and where is Stephen. With tears in my eyes i said to her he got five months in prison, she replied oh darling come here i was crying so much my heart felt so empty, i felt like my whole world was caving in around me, my heart was always so full of pain since mum died i just wanted my mum's arms around me so i could feel safe agaain. I have two children and their biological father abandoned his own two children. He chose a life of crime, drugs and being with his mates over being a good loving responsible father to his own children, it was hard being so young looking after my two kids being mummy and daddy to them both. Trying everyday to be the best that i could be for my three younger siblings, mum's wish meant everything to me and i never wanted her to look down on me and feel disappointed in me. What i did with my life after mum past away, I always wanted her to be proud of the person i was and i wanted nothing more than to carry out her wish. To be there for my younger siblings and that wish i was going to see through right till the end. The hardest part about losing my mum was when i was out, seeing other mothers and daughters being together, that was so hard for me. I could not walk past them in the street without wishing it was me and my mum and the thought my children would never know their nanny. My mum had missed out on so much, she missed out on watching her own three younger children grow up she missed out seeing all her grandchildren. She missed out on so much dying so young. I always asked mum when i was talking to her by her grave stone, i hope i get to see my children grow up mum whatever happens to me after that is in god's hands. The first night Stephen got sent to prison i laid awake for hours just thinking of the month we spent together, so that night i needed to be close to my children as my younger siblings were coming around the next day, So me and my two children slept in my bed that night and we cuddled up till we all went to sleep. The next morning my daughter asked me where Stephen was so i asked her to come and sit on my lap, i began to tell her that Stephen had been a bad boy, he had done some bad thing's before we all fell in love with him that he shouldn't of done and that he had to go away for a while, but he told me to tell you that he loves you very much and that he will send letters everyday to us all and that Stephen will be coming home soon, my daughter took the news of Stephen being away the best that she could, she was still very young and my son was not even talking at this time so he didn't really understand which was not such a bad thing. My life felt empty, my dad dropped off my siblings later that morning and right away my younger brother asked me where Stephen was so i told him the same as i told my daughter and he replied i 'm going to miss him. I said i know my darling but we will all be together soon. We had a good few days whilst we were all together, i had to make the best of my life for the time being till he would be home again, it was hard for me because i had five children to take care of and i never wanted them to see me sad so i had to hold as much back as i possibly could. Then when they were all asleep i could have my time where i could just let the tears and pain just flow, it was my release to be able to carry on with another day. When my dad picked up my younger siblings me and my two children went down to see my mate who i use to share the flat with, i was only there for a while, then on my way out i was standing at the top of the stairs of my mates flat when suddenly i looked down and there stood Stephen saying i 'm home babe. I couldn't believe what i was seeing. Stephen came running up the stairs hugging me. Then he told me he had done a runner from prison. I didn't know what to say i was frozen in shock. We made our way back to my flat, my little girl was so happy to see him. We sat talking and he told me he had to get out of there as it was too far for me to come visit him. I was in disbelief at what Stephen had just done, i had mixed feelings about seeing him because i had left my children's dad because i wanted my kids to have a better life than this, me and the kids were moving in two days time into a three bedroom house. I was so angry with him at the time even though it was good to see him, but not under these circumstances, it just meant more complications for us all, but he was here now and i didn't want to let him go. We were due to move into the three bedroom house that my dad had found me so we spent that day packing up all our belongings and the next day we moved in to our new home. As time went by life pretty much went back to normal it was like nothing had happened with Stephen going to prison, but everyday that went past i didn't know if that was going to be the day the police came knocking on the door to arrest Stephen and send him back to prison. So we just took each day as it came. The more time i spent with Stephen the more we were falling in love with each other. No matter what he had done in the past, i still found in my heart he was a good person and that all he wanted was a family of his own, when we were all together we felt like a family but i always reminded myself that one day the police would find him. We didn't go on the run as i had already been through that with my children's dad and was not going to go down that road again, so we just tried to live as much of a normal life as we could. We both treasured every minute of the days we had together, then just when things were going as good as they could do considering the circumstances life got even more complicated for us as my children's dad was now out of prison, as soon as he got out he was giving us trouble day after day, he just would not leave me or the kids alone. He would always use the kids as a reason to get to me. This went on for weeks he kept on saying he wanted to see his kids, so i decided to take my two children out to see their dad at his mum's house. I was only there for an hour because all he wanted to talk about was me and him and i wasn't there for that, i was there so he could see his children. Just as i was leaving his mum's house he shouted out i hear your new bloke is wanted by the police for doing a runner from jail, i might just give them a ring and laughed. As soon as me and my kids were back on the bus on our way home i phoned Stephen up and told him to get out of the house in regards to what my children's dad had said. But Stephen replied i 'm not running anymore if the police come then they come babe. Once we got home Stephen started to cook us all tea then suddenly there was a knock at the door, i opened up the door and two policemen stood there and asked me where Stephen was, with that i could hear dogs barking in my back garden. I got hold of my two children and made my way to the garden to hear a policeman saying just come out son it's over, then i saw Stephen coming out of the shed and just stood there waiting for the policeman to put him in a set of cuffs. Stephen then asked if it was ok for him say goodbye to me and the kids first, the policeman replied go ahead, Stephen bent down and gave the kids the biggest hug and told them he loved them and then he looked at me and said with tears in his eyes i am so sorry for doing this i just didn't want to live my life without you and the kids. We hugged and kissed and once again said our goodbyes to each other, the policeman then put the cuffs on and said lets go, as they walked him to the police car Stephen was still looking behind at us while me and the kids stood at the front door he shouted out i love you all, with tears rolling down his face i shouted back we all love you to and we will see you soon. The police car slowly drove away from us with Stephen blowing us kisses from the back of the car window saying i love you all and waving goodbye at us. I watched the police car until i couldn't see it anymore, then i shut the front door. My daughter asked me where Stephen had gone so i told her he had to go away but he will be back home soon and she smiled and started to play with her brother. I stood in the kitchen with our tea still in the oven and four plates sitting on the kitchen table, i felt so empty i knew who had called the police and was so angry because it was his way of getting Stephen out of the way so he could try to get back into my life again. I put the kids to bed and then sat on my bed running things through my head, things like what i am doing to my kids. I knew i felt so much for Stephen and i didn't know why but i knew once Stephen had served the rest of his sentence that we could be really happy together. I know to everybody else, in their eye's they thought Stephen was no different to the father of my two children, where Stephen had been into crime the same as my ex partner was, but to me there was a difference the father of my children did his crime when he had his daughter and i knew things were never going to change for him. He was to set in his own ways and i had to walk away, i had been with him for seven years and he was getting worse. If your own children can't make you change your life then nothing will, but Stephen was different he had done his crime before we met each other, i knew i was taking one hell of a risk after not knowing Stephen very long but i looked past the crime and saw nothing but good in him and my kids loved him. He was great with them as soon as he moved in with me he use to get up in the night to feed my son, he would help around the house but most of all i felt safe whenever we were together.

I was so sad after Stephen had gone back to prison i hit such a low point again in my life. It felt like i didn't know whether i was coming or going, there was no stability in mine or my kids life's and i hated myself so much. I never wanted my kids to get hurt i just wanted the best for them and most of the time i felt as if i had failed them. My anger got the better of me and i decided to phone up my ex partner and tell him that i knew it was him that had phoned the police on Stephen but he denied it and then said did they catch him then, I replied you know they did and in a rage i put down the phone. A few hours had past and my ex partner had made his way to my home, he said all sorts of things. I was scared of him as he had hit me a lot in the past, after a lot of arguing i repeatedly asked him to leave and finally he did go. From that day onwards he continued to hassle me day after day, this went on for a long period of time, at one point when i had my younger sister staying with me he somehow made his way into my home. We began to argue and he was starting to get really angry and out of the blue he just came towards me and told me he was going to kill me, with his hands around my throat he was trying to strangle me, i was choking and my face was going blue trying to catch my breath, when suddenly my little sister standing there crying and screaming at him saying you're killing her, she was kicking and punching him trying to get him off of me, then with a sigh of relief my ex partner just let go and i dropped to the floor. My little sister was still very upset and was hugging me asking if i was ok, he replied go get her a drink of water, my sister replied you go and get it you just tried to kill her. He came back and gave me a sip of water and said i 'm sorry, i just replied just get out of my house and then he walked out of the door. I was still on the floor in my hall way with my sister by my side. We just hugged and cried together. He continued to hassle me for weeks sometimes he would show up while i was talking to Stephen on the phone and in a rage he pulled the phone line out of the wall and smashed the phone to bits saying talk to him now without a phone. All this was happening in front of his children, me and my children went to visit Stephen in prison and on the way home as i came out of the train station i saw my children's dad waiting at the train station. I asked him what he wanted and he replied you've been up to see him with my kids haven't you, i replied yes i have. He said my mate is in the car we will give you a lift home as i want to see my kids, he was really angry so i just walked towards the car and me and my two children got into the back seat of the car, With my son on my lap and my daughter sitting by the side of me my ex partner then got into the back seat of the car with us. Out of the blue he started shouting at me and was getting more and more angry. I shouted back at him saying stop your doing this in front of the kids, with that he pushed my head against the back of the car window and started punching me several times in the face, my little girl was screaming and my son was on my lap screaming to. Then he stopped and said you deserved that you dirty slag, then suddenly the car stopped and we were outside my house. I got my children out of the car and started to walk towards my house, i was trying to put my key in the front door when he stood behind me and said i 'm sorry i never meant to do that, i replied get away before i ring the police, he started to walk away saying sorry. Once i got in i shut and locked my front door. I sat on the floor trying to calm my two children down my little girl said mummy your eye. She stood up and got a flannel trying to wipe away the blood from around my eye, after a while i managed to calm my children down. I gave them their tea then bathed them and put them to bed i then went into the bathroom and looked in the mirror to see that i had a black eye with a few cuts around my eye. I just sat on the floor of the bathroom and cried, suddenly the phone rang and it was Stephen, he ask me straight away babe are you ok. So i explained what had just happen and he replied wait till i get out on my day release, he's not getting away with this, i was crying saying i was ok then his phone card started to run out so he said i love you and the kids and i will phone again tomorrow then the phone went dead. Stephen phoned me the next day and told me they had cancelled his day release as one of the prison guards had over heard our conversation as they were listening in on our phone call. They heard Stephen saying he waits till he gets out on his day release, so he had lost it. There was nothing we could do, Stephen was angry because he couldn't do anything to protect me while he was in prison, we talked for a bit more until his phone card ran out and i told him that i would see him the following week for a visit. I had my younger siblings throughout the following week I couldn't hide my black eye because as the days were passing the bruising was coming out more around my eye. My brother asked me what i had done and i just told him that i had fallen over, me and my younger siblings done a lot together through the week, they went back home on the Thursday as i was going up to see Stephen the next day, So me and my kids went to bed early that night. We all got up and made our way to the train station. My children were in the play room when i went in to see Stephen as i knew we would be talking about what my ex partner had done that night. I walked in to the visiting room and Stephen just looked at me with shock on his face, i tried to cover my black eye up the best i could with makeup but it was still very badly bruised. I sat down and Stephen hugged me and said i can't believe what he has done, we sat talking about what happened and that Stephen only had eight weeks left to do of his sentence then he would be home, but for the both of us eight weeks couldn't come fast enough. My children came in to see Stephen for the last half an hour of the visit as they had really missed him. When the visit was over we all said our goodbyes then me and my kids made our way back home. That night after speaking to Stephen on the phone, he phoned me every night from the prison which made the time go a little bit faster in a funny kind of way, Seeing Stephen once a week and talking everyday helped us both get through the days. It was so hard for me as everyday my ex was still hassling me day after day, i would get a bit of a rest from him for a few days here and there hoping he had gone away for good then out of the blue he would just appear again. My life was hell, i spent many nights thinking of my old life when mum was alive we were such a happy family and i missed that more than anything, i never imagined my life would have turned out this way, i had so many plains as i was growing up but after the death of my mum everything changed for us all. I missed mum so much it would hurt so bad, i had my mum in my life for sixteen years and losing her like we did i found it so hard to move on with my life. I knew my life had to go on and that mum was no longer a part of my life anymore, but i just didn't know how to let her go. I would think about her everyday, about all the good times we had, then i would feel so sad because i always tried to imagine how my mum must of felt knowing she had cancer when my three younger siblings were so young and that she would never be there to watch them grow up. Being a mum myself now i don't think i could of coped with knowing that i had cancer and my children would not have their mum in their life's anymore. I always write in my day to day diary year after year everyday about what was going on in my life, i found it easier to express how i felt rather than talking about it to anyone. We all watched how hard my mum tried to fight cancer but in the end the cancer beat her, from the day we lost mum i started writing on a daily basis about my mum and that one day i would love to write a book about her after she had died from cancer, she was the best mum in the whole world and i didn't want my mum's memory to die in vain. As time went by stephen's release date was just around the corner, we only had two more days to go and Stephen would be coming home, Me and my children spent the day cleaning the house getting it all ready for the big day, we had missed him so much and knowing he would be home the next day we couldn't wait. He had served his sentence and when he was home he was free and we could start our lives with a fresh start. I got the kids ready for bed my daughter was so excited knowing we were going to meet Stephen in the morning and that he was coming home with us for good, but my son didn't really understand as he was only ten months old. When my kids were finally asleep i just stayed awake all night, i just couldn't believe he was coming home. I watched the sunrise early in the morning and started to get myself ready, then my daughter got up and said mummy is Stephen coming home today with a smile on her face, i replied yes my darling he is and he is never leaving us ever again. We hugged and then i got my children ready, we made our way to the train station for one last time and that felt so good. The train finally pulled at the station and my heart started to skip a beat as i knew once we got off the train Stephen would be waiting for us. So as we got off of the train we walked towards the waiting area and there he stood with his arms out, with that my daughter started running towards him and Stephen picked her up it was a picture, then me and my son walked closer to Stephen and we all just hugged with tears of joy, we were together again at last, with that Stephen said come on lets go home. Being all together on the train on our way home felt like heaven, we could all be together now with nothing standing in our way, somehow for me it felt almost too good to be true, trying to remind myself that the last three and a half months was finally over and that Stephen was home for good. It took a while to sink in for the both of us. Having Stephen by the side of us on the train felt so good and at last i felt safe again, my daughter looked so happy so did my son. My little boy was all over him it was an enjoyable train

ride home. It was so different to all the other times when me and my
children caught the train, going up to see Stephen in prison, i felt so sad
there and back, this time i felt so happy to have him back in my life
again. We finally got home and we had tea, Stephen played with the
kids for ages, me and Stephen just kept looking at each other all
evening it was a look of love on both our faces. I can't put in to words
how much we both waited for this day to come. We went to bed so late
that night, when we went to bed it was funny as my little girl never
liked to sleep in her own bed even though she had her own room she
just loved being in my bed. She had been like that since my ex went to
prison when she was six months old because i always had her in my
bed with me and she didn't want it any other way. It was so sweet as
Stephen loved her as much as i did, the first night Stephen was home
she got in the middle of us both and talked and talked to her heart's
content, she had me and Stephen in fits of laughter with some of the
things she would say we had our son in bed with us to, talk about four
in the bed, but we wouldn't of had it any other way. When the children
were asleep me and Stephen went downstairs and sat talking, hugging
and saying how good it felt that we were back together again and that
we never wanted to be apart from each other again. Stephen then told
me he had something to tell me and it was that when he was in prison
he started to smoke cannabis because most days he felt like he couldn't
cope and that he still had some left. He said i had to tell you because i
always want us to be honest with each other, i was glad he told me but i
knew i had to say how i felt about it and that i understood that
smoking cannabis in prison helped him cope but i did not want that
around my children and that i loved him but he had to make a choice it
was either that or us. I didn't want that life style for me or my children,
I had been through it all with my ex and i just didn't want it anymore,
with that Stephen stood up and went up stairs then come back down
got hold of my hand, we walked into the bathroom and Stephen lifted
up the toilet seat and put the rest of the cannabis down the toilet then
flushed the chain and replied say no more, i am not letting you and the
kids go anywhere ever again i lost you all once when i went to prison.
So why do i need that when i have you and the kids, with tears in my
eyes i said i love you so much. I didn't know how you were going to
take it, whether you were going to leave i just didn't know what to
think, Stephen replied you and the kids are my life now and i will
never do anything to lose you or the kids i love you all too much with
that we went back to bed. The weeks flew by as we had my younger
siblings stay with us, we all walked up to see mum and sat by her stone
with a packed lunch, the kids were playing but life for me was still so

hard without mum, even being by her stone it still didn't feel real that she was no longer here and that i would never see her again, or doing all the little things we use to do, just things like going into town together. The more i would think about the good times the worse i would feel. Three months went past like a blow in the wind mine and Stephen's relationship was going great and the children were so happy, but it didn't stay like that for long as my children's father started to demand to see his kids. He was back to his old tricks again just wanting to stop me from having a life of my own. This went on for some time so i decided to get a solicitor to arrange for him to see his children, as time went by my ex had his first visit with our two children. My little girl really didn't want to go as she didn't even really know him, my son also didn't know him, for them it was like meeting a stranger off of the street, i never wanted to let them go but it was something we had sorted out between both our solicitors. He picked them up at nine o'clock that morning and they would be home at five, i hated letting them go i was so sad all day and found it so hard to take my mind off of them both throughout the whole day, me and Stephen tried doing what we could to make the time go quicker, we just wanted them back home so that we knew they were safe, five o'clock came and there was no sign of my children, it got to half past five and still no sign. So i decided to phone him and ask him where my kids were, i said to him they were supposed to be back for five, he replied they will be back when i say and hung the phone up on me, my heart was racing with anger it got to six o'clock and i said to Stephen if they're not back in ten minutes i am phoning the police, i knew he was doing this to get back at me in any way he could. Then suddenly a car pulled up outside, i looked and it was my children, i opened the door and my kids come running towards me and Stephen, their dad then said i am having them over night next weekend, i replied no you are not and with anger in his face he replied watch me so i just shut the front door. Me and Stephen sat in the room asking my children if they had fun, with that my daughter said mummy i have got to say a bad word to you, Stephen said that's ok darling what do you want to tell mummy, that's ok if it's a bad word you just tell mummy what you need to say darling. My daughter then replied, he meaning their dad as they never called him dad they always called him by his name, she went on to say mummy i have to call you a bitch and Stephen a cunt, she was so upset with this me and Stephen comforted her and then she went off and played with her brother. I said to Stephen i am going back to my solicitor tomorrow, i was so angry how could he get her to say such a horrible thing, if he could be this way to the children on his first visit with his children what more could he put them through. With that the next day i saw my solicitor and she advised me to stop access and that she would write to his solicitor in regards to this matter, once my ex partner found out about this it made matters even harder for me and Stephen. He continued to give us more trouble as he didn't want to fight for supervised access, so in the end he decided to walk away again. We got back on with our life's and once again when it was bed time with our little girl in the middle of us both she was talking away to us playing with Stephen, then she laid down looked at Stephen and said will you be my daddy. I had tears in my eyes as it just come from nowhere and Stephen said to her i would love to be your daddy, with that she said night mummy and daddy and laughed. My daughter was so intelligent for her age and she always knew what she wanted Once my son learned how to talk he naturally started to call Stephen daddy, i always wanted my children to know the truth when they were old enough who their real dad was and that Stephen was there stepdad. My daughter i think already knew who her real daddy was but she wanted her daddy to be Stephen as he was always there for her as a dad should be. Later on when my son got older we both told him that Stephen was his step daddy and told him who his real daddy was but he wouldn't have any of it. The only daddy he knew in his life was Stephen, they both loved him to bits and with them being his step children Stephen said to me the day he met me and we became a couple was the day he fell in love with me and my kids. So from that day on Stephen classed my children as our children. Life was going as good as it could get for me, as me and Stephen were trying for a baby and i always saw my younger siblings. They were such a big part of mine and Stephens life and for me the day mum died and i was taking care of them at our family home i stopped looking at them as my brothers and sister, because they felt more like my own children. I loved them as much as my own two children and for me in my own heart i always had five children. I had them so much they started to all grow up together and i wouldn't change that for anything, being so close to my younger siblings i have always felt a part of my mum around me and that if she was looking down on us hopefully she would feel happy to see us all together. As time went on with me and Stephen trying for a baby i finally fell pregnant and for the first three months i couldn't get out of bed i was so ill with this pregnancy, i was always being sick and feeling weak most of the time. I just had no energy and Stephen was great, he took such good care of me he took over the run of the house and our children and my younger siblings. It was a lot for him but he coped so well, i would always find myself watching him when i was laid in bed while he was cleaning our bedroom, i just felt so in love with him that one day i wanted to marry him and spend the rest of my life with him. There are not a lot of good men out there that would take on two children that was not theirs, so i always knew i had one of the best and i was never going to let him go. We were not only lovers we were best friends to but most of all he was my soul mate and that we would have a bond forever. We talked all the time about mum he would sit and listen to me for hours. Then we started talking about his past, i never knew what his life was like as he never really liked talking about his family much but one night he told me about his past. He told me that his dad had committed suicide when he was only nine years old, his dad had took his older brother to school one day as he normally did, he then put his bike under a bridge and kneeled down on a train track and waited till a train came towards him. He was hit at a high speed of a hundred and twenty five mph and was killed instantly. Stephen had come home from school at dinner time and his mum told him that his dad had died then sent him back to school. After his dad died his older brother started beating on his mum so Stephen started to beat his brother up to protect his sister and his mum. The law took his mum to court for Stephen not going to school and put him in care at the age of eleven for his own safety, but before he was taken in to care his mum had a boyfriend who used to beat him with a belt on a daily basis for a year. Stephen had phoned the police on him and the police had come to his house and spoke to his mum. Stephen wanted to press charges but his mum refused to press charges .From the age of eleven after being put into care his mum never visited him once. I was streaming in tears throughout what Stephen was telling me, it was upsetting him telling me about it after all this time we had been together he had kept this all to himself. He said he never liked talking about his past. I was in shock i couldn't believe all what he had gone through as a young child. Stephen went on to say i will never have my kids go through what i went through as a kid. I would die for my children. We had a cuddle and for days after Stephen had told me it played on my mind for a long time. Somehow with mine and Stephens past made us even stronger as a couple, even though it took a long time for Stephen to tell me about his past it made me feel special because he had never told anyone else about his past and i felt glad that he could share such a horrible childhood with me. Throughout my pregnancy i was slowly starting to be able to do more but as i was getting bigger i could hardly walk and Stephen was still doing pretty much everything around the house, i felt so bad as i couldn't help a lot and that Stephen was doing so much but he said he loved taking care of me and he did me proud. He was one of the best and i felt very lucky to have him in my life after having such a bad relationship with my children's father, he treated me like a queen and the more time that went by our relationship was getting stronger and stronger by the day. We were so in love everywhere Stephen was i was and we loved spending all our time together, we never argued not once and still haven't to this day. I still say we were chosen to be together the way we met, the way we never thought we would ever see each other again just everything about our relationship was perfect in every single way. Destiny is what got us together and maybe my mum and his dad had a little something to do with that. Months slowly went by with my pregnancy and as i was getting towards the end now i was so big where with my other two children i was nowhere near as big, i could still do everything for myself and i think that's why i found it so hard with this pregnancy because i couldn't do anything to help Stephen. I was missing my mum so much being pregnant this time as i had alot of thinking time, i was often thinking what it would feel like to have your mum with you when giving birth and seeing mum playing with my children hearing them saying nanny, i felt so blessed to have Stephen in my life but i always had an empty space in my heart where mum had been but no longer was. I don't think no matter what happens in my life that empty space will always be there until we meet again. One morning i was starting to get a lot of pain and my contractions were coming every five minutes so i knew it was time, Stephen phoned my dad to ask him if he would have our children and dad said yes, so we got them ready and made our way to my dad's. We told them soon they would be having a little brother or sister, we hugged them and said goodbye then off they went with my dad. My contractions were getting stronger and stronger, finally we made it to the hospital and i had my waters broken. It was getting on to late afternoon and then i felt the need to start pushing, i needed to have my baby before midnight as today was the 24th of august the day my mum was born. Suddenly after alot of pushing i could feel my baby's head, Stephen was great with the delivery, i kept on pushing and pushing but the baby was stuck, the nurses were shouting to get a doctor in here and was telling me the babies shoulders were stuck and the babe was getting distressed, they needed to get the baby out. I was so tired i could barely push all i kept doing was looking at the time. Suddenly i saw three doctors come in, me and Stephen didn't know what was going on. Then the doctor said we're going to get this baby out and with that all together i had three sets of hands trying to twist the babies shoulders round, the pain was so intense i was laying half way down the bed and with the twisting and pulling from the doctors i shot right to the top of my bed so fast. I then looked down and one of the doctors had our baby in his hands saying you have a gorgeous little baby boy, i looked at the time and our son was born at ten past eight on my mum's birthday. I was crying so much as i was so glad that my little boy was born on my mum's birthday, the nurse put my son in my arms and i said hi you have the same birthday as your nanny. Words couldn't explain how many mixed emotions i had, Stephen was crying to i said we did it babe. Stephen kissed me and then held his son in his arms for the first time tears rolling down both our faces and Stephen said i can't believe our son was born on the same day your mum was. With tears of wanting my mum more than ever now having our son born on that day, i think it was mum's way of saying to me don't be so sad now the 31st of march has been replaced with joy as it was Stephen's birthday and now you have joy in your life on this day to. I was always so low on those two days and i knew my mum was watching down over me, she wanted it to be this way for me so i could try and let her go but no matter what that space in my heart will never go away, its a special place were mum's memories are and those memories will live on inside my heart until it's my time. That night i stayed in hospital and Stephen stayed with me. My dad brought my two children up to meet their baby brother, when my daughter saw him she asked to hold him so i sat her on the bed beside me and placed him on her lap, afterwards my dad picked his grandson up with look of joy on his face. He then past him back to my little girl and she just smiled she looked so excited. I did the same with my son i could see in both their little faces that they were happy i just couldn't wait to get back home to be with all of my three children. We said goodbye to dad and our two children i was so tired after giving birth to our son and was glad it was all over, i had such a horrible pregnancy and couldn't wait to feel myself again. The next morning i got discharged from hospital and we all went home, dad dropped my other two children off and it felt nice to be home but i still felt so tired. A few days after being home i really didn't feel myself everytime i had something to eat i got a really bad tummy ache, i kept going to the toilet everytime i would have something to eat, i just didn't feel myself at all. This went on for weeks after i gave birth to our son so i went to the doctors and the doctor said you might be suffering with irritable bowel syndrome, sometimes it can be brought on after giving birth so he gave me some tablets to take and i went home. At that point i didn't even know what irritable bowel syndrome was, the short word for it was I.B.S. The doctors didn't even know a lot about it as not a lot of research had been done. A few more weeks had past and the pain was getting worse the tablets didn't really help much so the doctor said that he would send me up the hospital to have some tests done just to make sure that there wasn't anything else going on, so i came back home again and weeks went by waiting for my hospital appointment to come through. I was still in a lot of pain so i couldn't really do much with my children. I was worrying all the time about having the tests done to find out what was going on. I started thinking about mum and how she died i was hoping nothing like that was happening to me as i didn't know anything about I.B.S I just knew i didn't feel right. We all know our own body, weeks had been and gone and finally my appointment came through it was in two days time. I was starting to get really nervous and i kept saying to mum please don't let anything happen to me, the day came to go up the hospital and i had the tests done to check the inside of my bowels and also had a biopsy done, the doctor told me after the tests were over that he couldn't find anything wrong everything looked fine but we took a biopsy just to be on the safe side. We went home as Stephen came with me i didn't know what to think i had to wait five weeks for the results of my biopsy and i wasn't getting any better, as time went by i found myself worrying so much more. I just didn't like the way i was feeling and it scared me, i just kept thinking i had something serious and kept thinking about mum. My mind was working overtime waiting for my biopsy results, then at last i phoned up for my results and everything came back normal i felt a great sense of relief that it was just I B S, but i still found myself worrying. My way of thinking was getting out of hand, i still didn't feel myself and i was told that i had I.B.S but knew so little about it. I didn't have any real support off of my doctor about how to deal with this condition, i felt really alone with it, as time went by i had to go back to the doctors again and was sent back to the hospital to have a laparoscopy done. They checked all inside my tummy and once again my results came back clear, i didn't know how to deal with what was happening to me or how to cope with this I.B.S. It felt like it was taking over my life, i went back to see the doctor once again and the doctor told me i was suffering with anxiety and depression he wanted to put me on anti-depressants, i took one of the tablets that day and i didn't like how it made me feel so i didn't take any more. Stephen once again started to take over the run of the house, looking after our children and my younger siblings when they came to stay. My life was such a mess i didn't know what was going on in my mind, i almost convinced myself i had cancer and that i was going to die just like my mum did. I found it hard to sleep as i was worrying day and night, this went on for months. I paid little interest in Stephen, my children or my younger siblings. No matter how many times the doctors told me that there was nothing wrong with me, i just had it in my head they were wrong and that i had cancer and was going to die just like my mum did. I knew i had a fear of cancer, i was crying a lot about my mum as i was missing her so much. A lot had gone on in my life since mum died. I had lost my granddad which was my mums dad when my youngest son was only three so i never really had the time to grieve over mum with everything that had gone on in my life, grieving is a process you have to go through and everybody finds their own way of dealing with their grief and you can't compare your greif to anyone else's it is something that is uniquely yours, trying to understand that where there is love one day there will be grief and where there is life there is death. Trying to deal with this each and everyday has filled me with terrible grief and watching the rest of my family get on with life made me feel i was facing the loss of mum on my own. I think that had a lot to do with my depression. Things were not getting any better for me so my doctor referred me to St Clements where i had to have group therapy to learn how to manage my depression. Having the I.B.S then dealing with the anxiety and depression was a dramatic personal change for me in my life. I dealt with having depression and anxiety for two years but i beat it drug free. I was convinced that after my treatment i had defeated my fear of cancer, it had been a terrifying experience for me. Most of the time i felt i was losing control of my own mind and my life but after two years of fighting anxiety and depression it felt good to feel almost normal again. I had lost out on so much time with my children that i could never get back, i could not of beat the anxiety and depression without the support of Stephen but now i was back in control of my life. For me it was a good place to try and start to rebuild my life and start to enjoy my life with Stephen and my children. I wasn't cured from my depression completely as everyday i had to learn to change my way of thinking, i would still have some days where it would show itself but i put all my thinking time into my children. I found that having too much thinking time was not helping me, so i had to find my own way of coping and finding what was good for me and what wasn't. Life after my depression was starting to look more positive. Stephen and i decided to get married on his birthday and the day mum died, we wanted to fill that day with happy thoughts. The day we got married was a really happy day for us we didn't have anything big we just got married in a registry office as we didn't have a lot of money but we were just happy to be husband and wife and all our children had the same sir name as Stephen which made us feel like our family was complete. Our children were all at school now and my younger siblings weren't so young anymore, they were starting to all grow up, we still had them stay with us as much which was lovely as they were still very much a big part of our life's and our family. In my heart they were still my children as much as my own. My dad got me my first dog and it was a gorgeous little Shitzu. It was a little girl and she was only six weeks old, my dad had got her from a close friend of his. Their dog gave birth to seven puppies and she had named them all after the seven firemen from the children's programme trumpton town, her name was dibbles she was black and white. When my dad first brought her round she was so tiny, our children were upstairs when dad dropped her off. After dad left i went upstairs and told our children to close their eyes as i had a surprise for them, i then said you can open them now and my little girl was so happy she had a smile that lit up the room, the boy's loved her to it was like a little play mate for them, they would not leave dibbles alone. Having a dog i think makes a family complete and she brought a lot of happiness into all our life's, now our children were getting older and were all at school me and Stephen decided to both get ourselves a job as we had been on social security for a long time. Stephen and i had both past our driving tests and wanted more out of life for our kid's as they never really had a lot growing up all they had was what we could afford. Most of all they always had love and stability in their life's and to us that was the most important thing in a child's life, we felt as parents we wanted them to have so much more in life so i got a job working in a hair salon doing hair extensions, as before mum died i had always wanted to be a hairdresser and with me having them myself for years one day my hairdresser offered me the chance to learn how to do them. I had known her and her daughter for a long time as my hairdresser and was so happy when she asked me, i replied i would love to so she said you can start tomorrow then, Stephen got himself a job as a multi-drop driver so our life's were starting to come together. The kids seemed to be a lot happier as we could take them for days out and me and Stephen felt like we were providing for our own children and not the government, we felt like we had a purpose in life. I found myself thinking a lot about mum still as being at work it was run as a mother and daughter business, and they were so close. It took a lot of getting use to as i would find myself just wondering off in my mind wishing it could be me and my mum. I would still have my low days missing mum but i always went to her grave side once a week to clean her stone and sit with her for a while, it was my way of coping with life without mum. I started to see my nana a lot as she was my mum's mother, my nana had never got over losing her daughter so young, she would alway come and see us once a week me and nana use to love just sitting there talking about mum. As time went on we ended up getting another dog it was another little girl and she was a Lhasa apso, she was only six weeks old and dibbles loved having a little play mate. The kids loved having two dogs i did to as i have always loved dogs so our family was getting bigger. I never wanted anymore children after having my last son as my pregnancy was so horrible it put me off of ever having anymore children. I was still suffering with my I.B.S as i had a sugar and yeast intolerance so i had to always watch what i had to eat which was hard to live with. At times it would get me down because if i had eaten anything that i shouldn't of i would be really ill and in alot of pain, stress would also bring on my I.B.S so at times it use to get me really down because sometimes i would be doubled up in pain. It would cause me to have chronic diarrhoea one day and then i would be constipated the next. When it was really bad i would be in bed for days but it had become a part of my life now so i had to learn to cope with I.B.S the best way that i could. Life for us all was starting to come together i was enjoying work it took away so much thinking time that i had over mum because reality was sinking in more and more that mum was gone but for me never forgotten. It's hard to understand there was a reason for all of this and one day it would become clear, i had to tell myself sometimes that i can cope with life and not fall apart that was my goal and finally i had accomplished it. Me and my hubby both having jobs we had the opportunity to do so much more with our life's and that made a big difference to the both of us, more so for my hubby as he felt like he was supporting his family at last. Life continued to stay stable for us i would still have my bad day's worrying sometimes whenever i fell ill and whether it was anything serious, i tried my best to shake it off and most days it paid off. Somedays i wouldn't be so lucky but it never took over my life as it did before. I knew what i aimed for and that was being a good mother to my children and a good role model for my siblings. I didn't have them in my life everyday like i did at the start after mum died but i made sure that they continued to be a big part of my life and that they always knew i was there for them if they needed me. After being with Stephen i started to become confident in myself again i had lost so much of myself after the death of mum and spending seven years with my children's father, i lost the person i use to be but finally to my amazement i was getting part of me back again, i never thought that would ever be possible. Depression was now a thing of the past for me and i was determined i had seen the last of it as life now for us all as a family we were inseparable. We ended up getting two more dogs both Lhasa apso's so in total we now had four dogs i had developed a passion for dogs since dad had got me my first dog.

All of them were growing up with our children, they all had their own little personalities and the children loved having them in their lifes. I had got really close to my nana after my granddad died as she was living on her own. She was still living in the flat they had shared their life in but she now felt it was no longer suitable for her being on her own as it was just too big, so she moved into a smaller flat on her own. It was in a place where other old people were so she had support of carers if she ever felt she needed help. She was still extremely independent but hubby and I decided to decorate her flat out for her to make it feel more like home, nana became a bigger part of our lifes. Our daughter was now 14 years old and our two boys were twelve & ten. Our daughter had always been bullied throughout her school life on and off but when she started high school she was starting to change. She had got into the wrong crowd and was going off the rails, she never wanted to be at home much anymore she always wanted to be out with her friends, her personality started to change. She completely changed as a person she was drinking smoking and speaking to me and her dad with very little respect. I was so set back by this and it was hard for me to accept her talking to me in such a horrible way. I no longer had my mum and would have give anything to have her here i knew i could never have spoken to my mum in this way. For me my daughter didn't realise how lucky she was to have a mum. Her behaviour got out of hand this went on for continued period of time and it felt like we were losing our daughter. We tried grounding her but she was determined this was the life she wanted to live and whatever we tried to do it just back fired on us. Our family was being torn apart and she was getting more out of control. Her behaviour was so over powering it felt like my heart had been ripped out, where had our little girl gone? She wasn't doing this for attention as she had plenty of that, i blamed myself sometime for the way she was as i never let her go out with her friends. Being a mum i was scared to let her go out as i felt as long as she was with us we knew she was safe. So i held on to her for as long as i possibly could. When i finally did let her go out to her she felt free to do as she wanted without her parents there to tell her off. It got to the point where we did not know what to do we just couldn't control her anymore. My I.B.S was getting out of control again and i just felt i couldn't cope, everyday was getting worse everything we tried to do just didn't make any difference. I was at work and i would get a phone call to say she was drunk and walking in the middle of the road, me and her started fighting we had always had such a close relationship and i couldn't bair to think i was losing my daughter, she was my life. I felt so helpless i just didn't know how to get my daughter back. It was destroying me seeing the way she was, it just wasn't our little girl anymore. I had the biggest ache in my heart i was convinced we had lost our daughter. She just continued to believe as long as she had her mates she didn't need us in her life so we were in a situation of not knowing which way to turn. We didn't even recognise her anymore and it was affecting the whole family. We had to make a heart breaking decision and made her stay with my sister as she wasn't so young anymore, it was the only thing left for us to try and that was to step back out of her life and hope for the best that she would come to her senses. It was a risk we had to take. Our daughter had tried taking an overdose and that broke our hearts we knew she had reached a desperate time in her life where she was just crying out for help as her and her boyfriend had split up, she felt she had already lost her family and just didn't see any reason for living anymore. It was so hard on all of us especially me. I felt me and my daughter had such a good relationship before she had gone off the rails and to think how we were now was hard for me to accept. All i could hope for was that in time our relationship could grow and we could be as close to each other how we use to be. As time went by she did come to her senses and realised what she had done and were her life was heading so we took her back home where she belonged. It took a while for her to get back to the girl she use to be but she had learned by her mistakes and we had our little girl back again. Being her mum i was in such extreme pain, having to watch your daughter that you would die for turn into someone that you didn't even know anymore, but i was overwhelmed with joy that we could now try and put it all behind us and get back to being a family again. Whilst i was working realisation started to sink in that mum wasn't coming back and i needed to focus on something other than losing mum, the truth is it was just too hard for me to get my head around most of the time but working was challenging for me and i enjoyed what i did, that encouraged me to start doing other things like going out with nana we would always talk about mum alot and i really started to get to know my nana, not only as my nana but her as a person. I found that i could talk to my nana about anything and she would always praise me up for looking after my siblings and taking care of mum's stone. We had a great relationship and the more time we spent together the more closer we were getting. With our children being at school and both of us out at work, Stephen and i found that our days were filled up with work and our nights were filled up with us being a family. Mine and Stephens relationship continued to blossom and we were falling more and more in love. We always made decisions together, we never argued and before we got our jobs we use be together 24/7 and loved each other's company. We were just completely head over heels in love and i was blessed to have such a great man in my life that had always put me and the children first before anything else. Our boys in school holidays use to love going to work with their dad even the dog use to go sometimes. Now we were both working we where able to go away on our first family holiday, we hired a motor home and we went to Devon for a week. We went to all the same places where mum and dad took us as kids and it was the best holiday ever as it brought back so many happy memories for me, we took all the dogs along with us to. The scenery out there was out of this world we went to monkey world as i had always watched their programme on T.V and wanted to meet Charlie and i couldn't believe it when i got to see him face to face, it was such a great holiday i had pictures of mum, me and my older siblings when we were all little, my dad had taken photos of us all in different parts of Devon. So we decided that we would do a photo album of our family in all of the same places, the kids loved it so much we didn't want to come home, it was a holiday we would always remember. We had been living in privately rented houses for as long as i could remember, we had moved so many times over the years and i had been waiting for my own council accomodation since i was 17 years old. When i was in the homeless unit i had lost the right to a council house when my dad got me my flat and i had been on the move ever since. We finally decided to put our name's on the council list as being private had it's good point's as we could move around whenever we wanted to, but most of all we could choose what area we wanted to live and also the house we wanted to live in. One house we lived in we loved it was in a great area and was a really nice house, it was just across the road from where our children went to school i would watch them from my bedroom window at break time playing in the school play ground and it was a safe area where we would feel at ease letting our children play on the grass with their school friends outside the rear of our house after school. We were completely happy living there but we were unprepared for the shock that we were about to receive, we were told we only had 28 days to move out as the people we rented the house from wanted to sell the property. So the pressure was on for us to find somewhere else to live with a lot of searching around we managed to find another house still close to where our children went to school it was a big upheaval for us all. In time we got settled in our new home and just waited until we got our own council house. Work for us was still going great and our children were happy, i still saw a lot of my siblings but not as much as when they were younger as they were now getting older and were doing their own thing in life. Mine and nana's relationship was great we did so much together and being with nana i always felt closer to mum. We use to go up to see mum then i would take my nana shopping, nana was a big part of my children's life's as she was the only nanny that they had as my hubby never saw his mum. My children's fathers family never had anything to do with them throughout there life's and with my mum not being here she was the only nanny my children ever had in their life's, nana enjoyed spending time with the children as much as they did her. The father of my children would still show his face from time to time just to remind me he was still around, he spent more of his life in prison than he did on the outside but paid no interest in his children's life's what so ever. It never really affected our children at all as they had their dad, my two children had always grown up knowing the truth about Stephen being their stepdad as i never wanted to hide the truth from them, i didn't ever want my children to grow up thinking throughout their life that Stephen was there real dad then have their whole life turned upside down to be told suddenly that Stephen wasn't their real dad. I was determined from the start when me and Stephen first met my children would know the truth as my daughter never called her father daddy as he was in prison when she was young. When he was in our life's he was never at home anyway and as they started to grow up they always respected me for that. Mine and Stephen relationship was out of this world i had found my perfect partner i loved everything about him, his warmth his generosity and his passion for the way he made me feel he was so open about his feelings towards me. He was so passionate in expressing his love for me but most of all i could trust him more than any other man i had ever been with to him his family was his life. We had so much respect for each other. He really was my best friend and my soul mate. I'm sorry if this sounds too good to be true and you're reaching for the sick bag but i have kissed enough frogs in my life to deserve a prince, and i loved it that he knew me and understood me better than anybody else. I have my daughter to thank for that, because if she hadn't kept touching his hair that day on the train who knows where my life would be today. I will always stand by my saying that it was destiny that brought us two together. Months had come and gone and hubby finally received a phone call from the council whilst he was at work to say that there was a three bedroom house available if we wanted it. So hubby phoned me up and told me i was so excited. Our two boys were at chantry high school but my daughter was still at a different high school. The house they offered us was up chantry just yards away from the boy's school, so i drove down the street where they told us the house was but they wouldn't give us the door number so i was just looking around and to my amazement there was just one house that stood out from all the rest and i just knew it had to be that one, i phoned my hubby up and said i have just been down to look at the house and i think it's number 56. We had to wait a few days for a letter to come to tell us what the door number was, when the letter finally arrived to our amazement it said on the letter door number 56, they said it wouldn't be ready for a month as they had to empty the house and tidy it all up. We waited a few weeks then decided we would take a drive by the house to see what had been done, as we drove by we saw two council vans outside so we asked if we could have a quick look around and they replied yeh go ahead. So we walked through the front door and couldn't believe what we saw it was difficult to take it all in, the house was in such a terrible state it was dirty it looked a complete mess but we had to try and look past what it looked like and picture in our minds what the house could look like once we had decorated it, but personally we were convinced that the house needed so much work done to it that it would be impossible without having the money to do what needed to be done. We felt so distraught that the council were only going to do such little work to the house then the rest would be down to us. Our children were excited until they saw what the house looked like inside, our daughter replied mum we can't live here it's horrible so we were in two minds what to do whether to wait for another house to come along which could take months or even years before we would get another offer on a council house. So me and hubby sat down and talked and made our decision to accept the house. We both had good jobs so we decided to take out two separate bank loans of £15,000 each to enable us to do the house up the way we wanted it. Once we had got the money we started work on the house in between our jobs. We were confident and determined to get the house the way we wanted it to look, we had to start with an empty shell of a house and start from scratch. Everything needed replacing me and hubby had to be so motivated to make a difference and make this house our home, but the more we were doing to the house the more we felt it was never ending. After a lot of hard work with me, my hubby and our children working as a team the house really started to come together, to my amazement looking around i could see that it was all coming together and finally we could see a home and not just a house. We worked for three weeks straight to get the house liveable for us to be able move in and continued until we had reached our goal. After us all being physically and emotionally tired after all our hard work our home was complete and was ready to move in to. The nicest thing about all our hard work doing the house up was we did it as a family, we had moments where we all got completely fed up but once we had finished and we had finally moved in we were happy to know that in the end we ended up having a really nice home. Our two boys loved being so close to the school as i use to have to drive them to school from the other side of town, our daughter stayed at her school as she didn't have long before she left school. Things were now going good for us all after the move, i still had my bad days missing mum and time was flying by. Our daughter had left school now and had her own boyfriend, she had been seeing him for a long time whilst she was at school and seemed to be really happy with him its weird how time flies. One minute they're babies and the next they're all grown up and you find yourself asking where all the time has gone. Then one day out of the blue our daughter came home to tell me and her dad that she was pregnant it was a complete shock for us both as she was still so young but it was what she wanted and she was really happy. She didn't stay happy for long though as her boyfriend left her not long after she fell pregnant so she was left on her own. She was an emotional wreck as she was still very much in love with him. It was hard for me and her dad as we had to buy everything that the baby needed. We supported her throughout her pregnancy and ended up getting her a flat of her own and it was a hard time for us all. At times she would fall apart with her boyfriend not wanting to know her or their baby, as parents you do what you have to do and stand by them. We were both only 36 years old and were going to be grandparents that took alot of getting use to. When i saw my nana i told her about my daughter being pregnant and that she would be a great great nanny. My nana thought alot of her granddaughter but she wasn't happy to hear that she was having a baby. She said she was too young but in time hopefully nana would feel different. My nana and i still saw each other at least once a week sometimes more, if she needed to go shopping or if she needed to be dropped off at my aunties for the day i would then pick nana back up and take her home. She use to come to ours on boxing day every year as Christmas day she would go to my aunts, nana always use to go to my aunties on Christmas day when mum was alive and then be with mum on boxing day. We loved having nana round on boxing day as she use to make us all laugh, once we were watching rocky on the T.V and when the film had finished she use to fight with the boys and make out she was rocky, i loved my nana to bits. Whenever i use to take her out for something to eat we use to always argue about who was paying and most of the time i would win as i liked paying as it was nice just to get her out of her flat for the day but sometime she would get so angry with me if i didn't let her pay and she would say to me i won't come out with you anymore if you don't let me pay so i use to have to give in to her and say OK nana you win. She was great whatever i did for her she would always be so greatful. She was always talking about mum saying how much she missed her and how she couldn't wait to see mum again. Then suddenly out of the blue me and hubby were on our way to a car boot sale one Saturday morning when i received a phone call of my uncle saying that nana had been taken into hospital early hours Saturday morning but for me not to worry as nana was not to bad. The doctors were just waiting to do some tests later on to find out what was wrong with her. I replied i will be with you in a hour and that i would meet them up the hospital, so with that me and hubby made our way up to the hospital. When we got on to the ward me and hubby walked over to nana's bed and i said hi nana you ok nana replied yes dear with her oxygen mask on her face, she asked me how our daughter was and how the two boys were, i replied they're fine nan. At first my auntie and uncle told us the doctors had done some tests and they thought nana had a water infection and wanted to send her home but my uncle said to the doctor how come she is in so much pain. The doctors then ran a few more tests and couldn't see anything wrong with her, so they ended up sending a specialist doctor down to check nana over and he knew straight away that there was something wrong with my nana's tummy. He replied we are going to have to take her down to theatre for an operation to try and find out what was wrong with her. We were told to go home and that the doctor would ring my auntie and uncle when nana came out of theatre, so me and hubby went from the hospital to go and see mum. I sat by my mum's stone and said you're trying to tell me something mum, you're coming to take nana. I couldn't put in to words how to explain what i felt that day, we left mum and went home to wait for my auntie to ring us with any news. It wasn't long before the home phone rang hubby picked up the phone and my uncle said that the doctor had phoned and they had got to go back up to the hospital and the doctor would speak to them when we got there, Me and hubby made our way up to the hospital. The doctor had told my auntie that nana had a diseased bowel and that her bowels where completely dead, he then said that they had given my nana about two hours to live. How could this be possible i kept asking myself it felt like someone had just stood behind me and ripped out my insides, i remember thinking to myself me and nana where only out together last week. I wasn't ready to let my nana go she was such a big part of my life and i loved her so much, nana was a sleep so i never got the chance to say goodbye just like mum. Nana always told me she was afraid of dying in case she never saw mum again but when i looked at nana's face i knew she wasn't afraid to die anymore. She knew it was her time to go be with mum, i felt such extreme pain in my heart that i knew i had to let my nana go. Even though i didn't get to say goodbye nana knew how much i loved her and how glad i was we had spent so much time together, when we were together we both loved every minute of it and that letting nana go she had left me behind with such great memories of our life together and that nana had waited so long to be with mum again. She had never got over losing her daughter so young and now nana would become an angel leaning over my shoulder whispering in my ear to let me know she was still here with me. Where ever i go i know nana and mum would always be around in their own special way. I went home as the hospital would only allow four people to stay and i wanted my auntie to be by her mum's side with the support of her family. I laid awake all night crying until i got a phone call off of my uncle to say nana had past away at ten to six on the morning of may 25th, So me and hubby left to go back up to the hospital so i could see nana and hold her hand for one last time. When i walked in the room where nana laid on her bed i had flash backs of mum and i just walked over to her kneeled down and took hold of nana's hand and said with tears rolling down my face i love you nana and as long as i live you will be in my heart with mum and i will never forget you. Life does go on we all know that is true but time doesn't always heal that heartache or take away that pain, but to our family who loved and lost you life would never be the same. Our children never got to know their nana and that was so unfair. Now my nana will not get the chance to meet her great great grandchild, i know someday i will be with my Nan and mum again but no matter what ever else i do in my life they will both stay in my heart. It is a very true saying that god really does only choose the best. After losing my nana my life felt so empty nana had been a big part of our family, my hubby never had a nan in his life but he loved my nan with all his heart, death didn't only take away my nana, death took away the only nana our children had in their life's to. After losing nana I found life really hard to cope with we went up to see nana at the chapel of rest it was what we did when we lost mum, when she died for me doing that somehow made it more real that nana had gone and for me it was my way of letting nana go. The day of nana's funeral was a hard day for everyone that loved her, we had to be thankful that nana didn't suffer and that had to be a blessing. She was with her daughter now and her husband and at long last she was at peace. As weeks past by i had another part of my heart that felt empty and i was finding it hard to deal with at times. I was scared because i felt i was getting depressed again and i never wanted to go back to that dark place in my life again. Me and my auntie started to get close i was glad of that as when nana was alive she said to me one day that she didn't know how her daughter would cope if anything ever happened to her as she would be all alone, my auntie had already lost her sister and her dad and now she had to deal with losing her mum, we got great comfort out of being with each other and over time we started to build up a good relationship. We started to see each other weekly doing all the things i use to do with nana, we would go up to the cemetery to see nana and mum together and in time my auntie became a big part of my life. Our daughter was getting bigger now with her pregnancy and started to see the father of her baby again they weren't a couple like before but they were talking a lot more. Hubby was still working and was offered the chance to go self employed it was better money than what he had been earning before so he decided to take the offer, i still had my hairdressing and a few more cleaning jobs so i was kept busy and hubby was to. I still saw my siblings on a regular basis and it was nice to see that their own life's where going well for them. My brother had his own daughter now and my sister had a son of her own. My youngest brother was getting on well in life. We had another holiday away just me, hubby our two boys and our dogs. Our daughter stayed with my sister as she didn't have long to go now before her due date and we didn't want to risk taking her along in case anything went wrong with her pregnancy. We phoned her twice a day everyday sometimes more. When we were away it felt good to get away after losing nana and being away from work, it was good to have a break. We got back off of holiday and a month went by then our daughter went into labour it was a hard labour for her. I was with her along with the babe's dad, after hours of pushing with a few complications our daughter finally gave birth to a gorgeous little boy weighing 5lb 15oz on the 8TH of December and he was beautiful, Me and hubby found it overwhelming that this lovely little boy was our grandson and that we were grandparents at the age of 36 it was a happy day we will always remember. Soon after our daughter gave birth to her son her and her boyfriend decided they would give their relationship another go and got back together and became a family. We were all at a happy place in our lifes at this point. We had a good Christmas with our grandson but i found it hard not having nana there on Boxing Day. Work was still going well. I still went up to see mum and nana once a week and was still seeing my siblings, i was at a point in my life where i could look back and hold my head up high as i had been a big part of my younger siblings lifes since mum died and i had done the best i could for them. The hardest part for me now as they were getting older was letting go of that motherly love that i had always had for them all these years. I do find myself thinking what it would feel like to have a brother and sister relationship with them as in my heart i had always classed them as my own children as they were a really big part of mine, hubby and our children lifes, my daughter had always said when she was growing up that they are your brothers and sister, but for me in my heart the day mum died i never had that kind of relationship with them and even my younger siblings say now they are older that they look at me as a kind of mother figure, it was hard but if i had to do it all over again i would do. I did what i did for my younger siblings out of my love for them but most of all i did it for my mum. It would have been a lot harder for me if i had to look after my younger siblings on my own throughout their lifes aswell as my own children but i would have done it no matter what. Meeting hubby when i did whilst i was having my siblings we just naturally became a family. Hubby and i knew all there school friends and met their girlfriend's and my sister's boyfriend. I hold all that close to my heart and when i go to mum's grave stone i can stand there and say MUM I DID IT. Mum's memories played a big part of my life to i think it's good to have memories but for me i didn't know how to let mum go, i held on to her memories so tight ever since i was 16 years old and as i grew mum's memories grew with me. The memories i had felt like a stone in my pocket weighing me down that i carried around for years and sometimes i would feel like i wanted to let mum go as i had held on to her for as long as i could remember but that is how i coped with my life without mum. Months went by and on the 8th of May to our horror hubby lost his job as the company he worked for had lost the contract he was employed on, with him being self employed he wasn't entitled to any redundancy and the company that took over the contract were not required to offer him employment. So hubby was out of work with no other prospects of employment he found himself lost not knowing what to do. He had contacted every other delivery company around but due to the recession nobody was employing they were having to let people go themselves.We had money put away that we had saved including hubby's tax money, we applied to the social to see if we were entitled to claim but was told because of the amount of savings we had we were not entitled to any help even though £7,500 of it was to be paid to the tax man. We both sat down and thought what other alternatives there was but the only one we could think of was for hubby to buy his own van and try to get some sameday delivery work. We ended up spending thousands on buying the van, luckily though hubby still had all of his insurance still in place then there was the cost of all the advertising which ran into hundreds of pounds. Whilst paying out for all this we still had to pay all our bills and the loans we had taken out for the house. After paying out for the van and advertising we hoped things would start looking up but no nothing hubby just couldn't compete with the prices the big companies where able to charge. It came as a big shock when i lost my job's to literally one after the other due to the recession. As time went by hubby started to get down as he was unable once again to provide for his family and this made him feel less of a man, he felt worthless. As money started to run low hubby was left with no alternative but to sell the van as he had to pay half of his tax by July, we had used some of the tax money to buy the van hoping we could make it back in time for hubby to pay his tax. After this things started to go downhill rapidly for us both, with all the worry and stress hubby started to get depressed and i started to get ill. At the beginning of July i started to feel really unwell at first i put it down to my I.B.S due to all the financial pressure we were under but as the days went by i was getting worse and the pain i was getting was different to what i normally experienced. So the next day i decided to go to the doctors just to get checked out, after the doctor had examined me, It turned out i had an acute kidney infection and was given a course of antibiotics and sent home, i was in so much pain it was something else i had to deal with on top of everything else.Within days the anxiety had kicked in and the worry that whether the doctor had got their diagnoses right or was it something more serious .Over the next few weeks my health was getting worse, i ended up getting a severe chest infection and within weeks of recovering from that i ended up with the flu .We were then struck with another blow of bad luck as our eldest dog the one my dad had brought me fourteen years ago had become seriously ill and we had to make the heart breaking decision to have her put to sleep as the vet said there was no other choice due to her age. At this point my anxiety had got as bad as it could have ever got i had never experienced it to this degree, not only was i dealing with the anxiety i had started experiencing panic attacks. All of this was affecting my health quite dramatically. My I.B.S was flaring up on a daily basis. Hubby at this point was getting more and more depressed as money was getting really tight and we were struggling to pay the bills and keep food on the table. Hubby took it into his hands to contact a debt consolidation agency to see if we could get our debts combined and reduced due to the circumstances we were in. They helped by contacting our creditors and getting our payments reduced to an amount we could afford. This was a bit of a releif but we were still struggling, hubby was still doing what he could to find work but with no real luck. All he was offered was work through an agency which wasn't garanteed, he never did get a phone call back from the agency. So we tried once again to get some help from the social luckily this time they were willing to help as we no longer had any savings left.We had to wait three weeks for an appointment but they wouldn't give us any money until we had this appointment. Hubby felt so degraded having to literally beg for help from a system that is supposed to be there for people when they are made redundant. Once hubby had his signing day he went and asked them what help they could give him to get back into work as my dad and brother were lorry drivers and if hubby had a class 2 license they could of got him a job with the company they both worked for, hubby explained this to the advisor only to be told that he wasn't eligible for any help until he had been signing on for at least six months, my hubby couldn't understand why. So he came away feeling even more depressed than when he went in. Hubby's moral had hit a real low i had never seen him so low in all the years we had been together he had always been so strong. Even our children were noticing the difference in him, his mood was so low and this was heartbreaking to see as he had always been my rock but i in myself wasn't strong enough to be able to help him. That horrible black hole was back i was now suffering with acute depression, anxiety and panic attacks. I felt like i just wanted to die i couldn't deal with these feelings again. I went to the doctors and they prescribed me tablets called Diazepam, I hated the thought of taking tablets as last time i beat it without the use of tablets but this time it was so much harder. I also asked for them to refer me to st clements which is where i got the help i needed before but they were reluctant to do so, hubby went mad at the doctor and lost his temper he said how the hell is she supposed to get better if you're not willing to refer her, the doctor replied the resources just aren't there now like they where the last time i suffered. With that hubby replied all it comes down to is money that you don't want to spend. After a lot of arguing the doctor finally agreed to send a referral. Within a few weeks we heard from the crisis team from st clements and they wanted to do a home visit to see what help if any they could offer me. When they finally done the home visit and saw what i was dealing with and how suicidal i felt they agreed i did require their help. An appointment was made for me to see one of the doctors at st clements. I had the appointment and was given a prescription for sleeping tablets and anti depressants. These helped to a certain degree but not completely, my health was still a concern. After a while i was allocated a case worker who would come and see me on a weekly basis to make sure i was getting the adequate care and to make sure things weren't getting worse for me, she suggested that C.B.T may be of some help to me to try and control the anxiety which at this point was out of control, she also expressed her concerns about hubby's mental state as that was deteriorating rapidly, he had so much anger built up due to the way he felt but he wasn't one for talking about his feelings to strangers, he has always been a private person and kept his emotions to himself which wasn't helping him but he would always make sure i got the help i needed regardless how he was feeling. I ended up being admitted into hospital in December 09 as my health was still deteriorating. They ran loads of test for crone's disease and other similar diseases with the same symptoms over an eight day period but they couldn't find anything so put it down to my I.B.S and discharged me on Christmas Eve but i knew there was something not right. Christmas day i spent the whole day in bed it was the first year we had not celebrated Christmas. I ended up back in hospital on 27th severely de-hydrated. I was unable to go to the toilet so they fitted a catheter and an IV to re-hydrate me, they monitored me over a forty eight hour period but still never found what was causing the pain. During the time i had been in hospital hubby had started to find it really hard to cope with his depression and his emotions and had started to smoke cannabis again. He was finding life really difficult to deal with he wasn't eating or sleeping, he was trying to keep everything together whilst trying to deal with his own feelings. He ended up having trouble with his gastric reflux valve so every time he tried to eat he was in severe pain he finally went to see the doctor who prescribed him some tablets to relieve the pain, they also gave him some sleeping tablets to try and help him sleep but they didn't really help him as he still couldn't sleep. Things weren't getting any better for either of us even though hubby was using cannabis he was feeling guilty using it but didn't know how else to cope. When his six months of signing on arrived he asked for help to get his class 2 license only to be told it was to expensive and they didn't have enough money in their budget to finance it so hubby lost it he felt so let down, he had worked for the past nine years and paid all his taxes but the last year he worked had been self employed and had in total paid £7.500 in tax and £2.000 in N.I.so why was he not entitled to help. This made him a lot worse his anger was getting out of control. It was never aimed at me or our children it was aimed at everyone else, someone would look at him and he would just fly off the handle. Things were getting out of control i tried convincing him to try and get the doctor to refer him to st clements to see if they could help him, he took a lot of convincing but finally he went to the doctors and got them to refer him. When he finally saw the doctor at st clements they diagnosed him with acute anxiety, depression and an adjustment disorder. The doctor prescribed him with clonazepam, metazapine on top of his sleeping tablets hoping they would help. They helped for a while but he was still not sleeping or eating properly he had lost three stone in a matter of six months. Our doctors were concerned about this and wanted to refer hubby to the hospital for some tests but hubby refused he just put it down to the stress of what was happening to us and the fact he wasn't eating. He would probably have a sandwich a day at most, sometimes nothing at all. Our financial state was getting out of control we were really struggling to get by so we decided that we would have no choice but to cancel the payments on the debts we owed. Within weeks of doing this we started getting letters from our creditor's threatening to take us to court if we didn't resume our payments so hubby rang them and explained the situation and told them how do they expect us to pay when all we get is £102 a week to live on, with that they gave us a three month grace period and would contact us after the three months to see if our circumstances had changed. Hubby was now seeing his doctor at st clements on a monthly basis the same as me, i was unable to carry on with the C.B.T as i wasn't in the right frame of mind to concentrate. On one occasion when i was seeing my doctor at st clements i mentioned to him that i had felt a lump on my right breast which felt like a gland, myself personally i wasn't concerned as i had always kept up with my smear tests and i had my breast check six years previously but he advised me to get it checked for my own piece of mind. So i made an appointment to see my doctor and she made an appointment to get it checked, she told me it may be a cyst but there is definitely a lump there so i had an appointment booked for 27th September at 9.30 2010. On the day of the appointment i was a bit on edge and my anxiety was quite severe but i wasn't really that worried as i had been through the tests before and they had always came back normal and with all the tests i had throughout the year going in and out of hospital, the amount of blood tests that i had i thought if there was anything out of the ordinary the hospital would of picked it up. My appointment day finally arrived so hubby and I along with my daughter went to the breast clinic and i was asked to take my top off along with my bra so the doctor could check the lump. She sent me straight down for a ultra sound, so i laid down on the bed with my eye on the doctor watching him doing the scan and the expression on his face told a lot he said you have three cyst's, he then started checking the same lump that i had checked six years ago but back then they only done a fine needle test and one biopsy which came back that it was a benign tumour. I was so scared back then my anxiety was bad for a month or so until i was told that everything was ok, after having such a frightening experience it took some time to put it all behind me. So with the doctor checking the same lump again it started to alarm me, i said to the doctor can i ask why you are checking the same lump that i had checked six years ago. At first he didn't reply so as i laid there with my heart pounding i said to the doctor i already know, the doctor replied to me what do you know? I replied i know that something is wrong. With that the doctor said all i can say is i am quite concerned about this lump i was then ask to get dressed and to go back to the breast clinic. We made our way back and waited to be called in i wasn't waiting long but to me it felt like hours. I was called in and was asked to sit down the doctor said i need you to have a mammogram done as we are just a bit concerned about that lump, so we all made our way down to the waiting room and within minutes i was called in, the mammogram was all over and done with within minutes. I was again told to make my way back to the breast clinic at this point i was starting to panic my heart was racing whilst we just sat there waiting to be called in. Then my named was called and we went in the doctor said we need to do a fine needle test and three biopsies if that is ok, the doctor didn't really give much away apart from telling me to try not to worry, So i laid down and had the needle test done first, then the three biopsies, i then had the three cyst's drained. I was then sent home, i didn't know what to think but i knew something wasn't right i just had a gut feeling, i waited for three days before i was called back up to the hospital for my results. My appointment was on the 1st October at 1 o'clock so we got up there for 12.30, it was so frustrating my mind was working overtime and the anxiety was starting to get out of control causing me to have panic attacks. Hubby's anxiety was going through the roof as well. My name was called and i felt like i was going to pass out i found it so hard to control my emotions and as i walked towards the doctors room it felt like my legs were going to give way, i still had this horrible gut feeling that there was something wrong with me. Once we had made our way into the room and sat down the doctor started off by saying that your results are back in and your biopsies have come back clear but the fine needle test that we did came back as showing some abnormalities, to our shock the doctor said we are looking at it being either breast cancer or radial scar. She then said that we need you to come back up on Monday 4th October at 2.30 so they could do an open biopsy i was told either way i would require surgery, so i was sent down to Foxhall day unit to fill in the paper work and have my bloods done i also had to sign a consent form for my surgery. Me and hubby walked out of the hospital and we felt like we had been hit by a brick wall, We were in complete shock i kept saying to myself this can't be happening to me, my emotions were going wild and once me and hubby had made our way back to the car i just broke down crying to hubby saying i' m the same age as my mum 38 years old. The same age mum was when she was diagnosed with breast cancer. Emotionally i was a mess i continued to cry all the way home my emotions were out of control. I was thinking what on earth is radial scar i had never heard of it and didn't think to ask the doctor when she was telling me as i just stepped back and went into my own little world once she said i needed surgery, it felt like a block off point for me because all i could think about was mum. Cancer was my worst fear ever since i lost mum and my worst fear may have come true. Mine and hubby's anxiety was so bad we both had to take more of our Clonazepam than we should do just to calm us both down. Once we got home hubby looked up on the internet to find out what radial scar was. We found out that only one in two thousand five hundred women were affected by this. Where a normal tumour is a solid mass radial scar is a combination of spike like tumours, the danger with this is a standard biopsy doesn't work as the spikes actually hide the cancer cells. With this i just went into complete shock being told this i felt like someone had just ripped out my insides, i just felt like i was an empty shell and i instantly started having suicidal thoughts of just harming myself. I had convinced myself that i couldn't go through with what mum had gone through i wasn't strong enough to cope with that, i was already depressed before i was told this and found life to hard to cope with as it was, i started smoking more and more at times i just sat there thinking how can this be possible. All my life since mum past away cancer had become a fear for me, a fear i thought would never come true. I managed to get through the next two days how i do not know but Monday was here, we got to the hospital early and at 2.30 i had the open biopsy done i was asked to return to the breast clinic on the 11th of October at 9.30 for my results and to discuss my options. We came back to the clinic on the 11th and waited to be seen by the consultant, I was called in to one of the doctors consulting rooms and was told by the doctor that i did have radial scar and that i would require a full mastectomy, my surgery had already been booked for the 3rd NOVEMBER. The doctor said it was a good sign as all my biopsies had come back benign so once my breast had been removed if there was any cancer there it wouldn't be much but if they did find any i would have to have radiotherapy but they wouldn't know for sure until the breast had been sent to the lab and analysed. I was told all this on the 11th OCTOBER only three days away from my daughter's birthday, on the day of her birthday i just couldn't bair to do anything with her like we use to my mind was just in a world of its own. Everytime i saw my kids and my grandson i started to cry because i wouldn't know yet if i had cancer or not, all i kept thinking of was watching my mum die of cancer at a young age of 16 and losing mum destroyed my life, you tell yourself things like this don't happen to people like me. Mum she didn't smoke or drink alcohol she never in her life did any wrong and she died at the age of 39 with seven children, four of us were older but my three younger siblings were so young that they would never know who their mum was and here i was at the same age facing the same as my mum.The difference was i lived to watch my younger siblings and my own children grow up and i even got to meet my grandson all of the things my mum didn't get to do. My youngest son was 16 years old the same age i was when mum died, my children never got the chance to have my mum in their life's the only nana they had ever known was their great nana and she was the best nana ever, god rest her soul. So i knew i had to somehow get through this and as long as i had my hubby and my children by my side i stood a small chance of beating whatever was ahead of us. I never wanted my children to ever feel the pain i felt when my mum died but one thing was for sure i was determined that my grandson would carry on having a nana in his life that my children unfortunately didn't have. I had three weeks and one day to go before the day of my surgery, i am crying and crying writing this page as three weeks feels like a life sentence to wait to find out if you have cancer or not, i had gone all those years trying to imagine how mum must of felt when she was told she had breast cancer. Now i know i feel my mum's pain now it's happening to me. Somedays were bearable where i managed to get through this, other days i found myself just wanting to give up because if i did have cancer i didn't want to know but i had to continue to get through the next three weeks. I also had to have another appointment up the hospital on the 25th of October at 4 o' clock as i had been referred by my doctor as i was continually getting urine infections and i had to have a camera put into my urinary tract i couldn't handle anymore bad news but luckily the doctor told me that i had a kink in my urinary tract and that it could be easily corrected with surgery but he wasn't going to do anything until after the surgery for my radial scar as he wanted me to recover from that first. So many times i kept saying to my hubby i can't do this but what i didn't realise was what i was going through he was to and it was affecting hubby just as much as me. It took a life time for us to find one other and we couldn't bair the thought of ever being apart. My daughter always spoke to me about how she felt and how scared she was, our two boys didn't really know how to cope with the situation they kept a lot to themselves. As the days were getting closer i felt i was getting stronger all i wanted was to get the surgery over and done with, hubby wasn't coping with it to well at all because when i do go in for my surgery i would be asleep but he would have to be the one sitting there waiting for me to come out of surgery, i can't say i would want to be in my hubby's situation. My younger siblings found this hard to deal with to as i had always been a big part of their lifes. Well the wait was over it was the 2nd November the night before my surgery and i was feeling really tearful, physically and emotionally drained but i had made it through the weeks, i was scared and overwhelmed with my emotions all the what if's kept running through my mind as i laid in the bath that night i looked at my breasts for one last time and knew the next time i looked at myself i would look different, as tomorrow they would be going to do the operation on my right breast and would be putting an implant in my left breast so that they could get a perfect match for my right breast once they had removed it as i was having a rebuild on the same day. I saw my daughter that night and my grandson i gave him such a big hug it broke my heart saying goodbye because with surgery you never know, he was only 2 years old so he didn't understand really which was good. I had a lot of support from my auntie and her family throughout all this as we had become so close, she was scared to as she had lost her sister through cancer and i was very proud to have her by my side, i had a phone call off of my best mate and text messages off of the family. My dad phoned me and we had a chat, he told me that he loved me and that he would be up the hospital when my surgery was done. Then after a few tears before i went to bed me and hubby got up at 4.30 in the morning as i had to be there for seven, we got up had a talk and a cuddle and dad phoned to say good luck, it was then time to leave. We said goodbye to our two boys and then set off up to the hospital, i didn't feel too bad once i was there i couldn't cry anymore as i had cried so much. I took a picture of my mum and put it under my hospital bed so i had her there with me, the doctor came in and told me the operation should only take an hour and a half so i looked at hubby as they were ready to wheel me down as i was first on the list, i said goodbye to hubby and told him i loved him with all my heart, hubby replied i love you to and i will be right here waiting until you come out and off i went to the operating theatre and was put to sleep. After my operation i was in the recovery room i looked at the time and it was 1 o'clock, i started to get a really sharp pain in my chest and as i looked down at my chest they looked really big a nurse said to me are you ok and i replied no this pain in my chest, with that the nurse shouted out to the surgeon she came over and said we are going to have to rush you back down to theatre as you have an internal bleed. So they rushed me back through to theatre i was in so much pain i could hardly speak but i managed to ask them to let my hubby know what was happening. With that i had my second load of anesthetic and was put back to sleep i woke up again in the recovery room and felt so ill. I got back on the ward at 6.15pm and i can't really remember much at first apart from hubby helping me to go to the toilet then i looked up and saw my dad there trying to speak to me with my older brother and his wife, i could hear my dad telling hubby to go home as he had been up there all day. He had been going out of his mind as i found out that one nurse came down to tell him that i had been rushed back to theatre but didn't explain why. He didn't know whether i had died or if anything had gone wrong, he was sitting up the hospital all alone with nobody to help him through them six hours. They had left him sitting there not knowing anything and with anxiety he was going out of his mind with worry, so hubby kissed me goodnight and said i love you. My dad, my older brother and his wife stayed with me and i will never forget the look on my dad's face it was a look of shock as i was in a pretty bad way. I was so frail and i could hardly speak still i felt like death warmed up, i couldn't wee so dad got the nurse in to help me. Dad then left and my older brother and his wife stayed with me for a while longer then they had to leave. Later on in the evening i got taken off the ward and was put into a room by myself as i started to come around i felt in so much pain but worst of all i felt so alone as they wouldn't let my hubby stay up the hospital with me. So i laid there in my bed and just cried i felt so angry that my operation had gone so wrong, i had three drainage pipes stitched in to my chest and they were hanging everywhere. I can honestly say the worst day of my life was when mum died the second was the day of my operation, words can't explain no matter how hard i try, i just felt like i wanted to die. I took the picture of mum out from under my pillow and just looked at her i felt so empty and i had no more fight left in me. I remember thinking i wish it was all over but i still had the not knowing yet if i had cancer or not, i found it so hard to accept the reality of what i had to have done. I needed a wee so i pressed the buzzer for a nurse to come and help me go to the toilet but i got no reply so i was struggling to get out of my bed but i knew i had to go to the toilet, i got out of bed and had to stand there trying to pick up all the drainage pipes and the bottles. I walked into the bathroom that was in my room and looked in the mirror i just stood there looking at myself, it didn't look like me so i went closer to the mirror and just stood there and started to cry, i felt angry sad and lonely so i lifted up my nightdress forgetting all about why i had got out of bed in the first place, as i slowly pulled up my nightdress feeling like any minute i was going to collapse i finally got to look at my breasts as i only had a the bottom half of my breasts covered where they had opened me up from the bottom of my breasts. I was completely unprepared for what i was about to see, as i stood there looking at myself in extreme pain i just froze like a block of ice. My right breast did not even look like a breast it was so sucked in by the tubes, i had nothing there i fell to the floor and just wanted my mum, that's all i wanted at that time. I was so uncomfortable and in so much pain, i felt myself getting so angry WHY ME, WHY i kept asking myself, i just wanted to die that night. I felt i had the life kicked out of me and i just wanted to say ok god you win i can't do this anymore, you took away my mum so why leave me here to deal with this, i just laid on the floor crying until a nurse came in, she said darling come on let's get you back into bed, so she helped me back to my bed and i just laid there and cried until i finally fell asleep. The next morning i woke up and i felt like i had been ran over by a bus or something of some sort, i could still hardly move and was still in complete shock after my operation. I tried to have a wash in bed but only managed my face and hands as i still found it so hard to move. My surgeon had come into see me and told me what had happened throughout my operation, she explained what went wrong and said she was glad to see that i was looking better than i did yesterday, she also said that in three months time i would possibly need another implant put in because of the internal bleed that i had. They had to cut me from the top of my breast across to near my under arm to enable them to get to the bleed. Hubby got up the hospital early and said i was looking a lot better we tried to have a cuddle but was impossible with the pain i was in and having all the tubes hanging everywhere. Hubby was telling me how he felt on the day of my operation and that he thought he was going to lose me and said he never wanted to feel that way again. As the day went by it got to six o' clock and i was allowed to go home and was told that a district nurse would come to my house everyday to check on the drainage pipes and to make sure everything was healing how it should be. It felt good to be back home, with all the tablets i was on plus the ones i was sent home with from the hospital i went off to sleep a bit better that night, being in my own bed helped and having hubby by my side after last night feeling so alone I felt at ease being back at home.

The following morning i had to have help off of hubby so i could have a bath and that was so painful, i had to have a chair by the bath to stand my three bottles on and just let the tubes hang over the side of the bath, I'll never forget sitting in the bath with the mirror in front of me just looking at my breasts, i think it was my way of accepting what i had done. I just found myself going into a world of my own, it was so hard as i felt really low anyway before my operation, afterwards i just felt as if i was in limbo. I was worried about my test results, what if i had cancer? I had already told myself if it did come back that i had cancer i was going to refuse any treatment as i didn't want my children to see me go through what i saw my mum go through trying to beat cancer, watching her being so ill after the treatment, being sick and having to be in bed all day in pain, seeing that when i was young i didn't wish that on my children so my mind was made up. I just tried to hold on to a little bit of hope that maybe i would be ok but after how much bad luck i had had in the last two and a half years i didn't hold out much hope that any good luck would come my way, so it was hard to know which way it was going to go. I started to feel a bit better as the days went by, i didn't feel so drained and i was starting to move around a bit more, i kept trying to help hubby by doing a bit of polishing around the house as i felt so horrible leaving everything for hubby to do, he always got mad at me and told me off and would always send me back to bed and say i needed to rest. On Sunday the 6th of November the nurse came round and i had two of my drainage pipes removed, i felt a lot better for it as i only had one left in my right breast as that was the breast i had to have rebuilt and where the internal bleed had been so that had to stay in for ten days and i had to go up to the hospital for that to be taken out. My days were getting harder as it was getting closer to the 12th November that was the day i would get my results back; i had reached a point now where the not knowing was worse than knowing one way or the other. I felt it was torture and i was going out of my mind asking myself if i had got cancer or not i just wanted to know, i couldn't get mum out of my mind thinking about how she must of felt and also how i was feeling in myself, my emotions were all over the place, i was having dreams that i had cancer and it would wake me up and within seconds i would start having a panic attack, i just felt i was losing all control of my own thoughts and i was losing the plot. I just couldn't take anymore so i phoned up the breast care nurses and spoke to her, i tried to explain how i was feeling and she told me that she would see what she could do to find out if my results were back and would let me know if they were, i felt a bit better after the phone call but it didn't last long before my anxiety kicked in again with all the worry of not knowing. Another day had past and it was the morning of the 10th of November a day i would never forget the phone rang so i picked up the phone and said hello, she said hi its Helen and i said hi with my body shaking all over as i knew it was for my results, she said your results are back and it has come back all clear you have no cancer, within seconds i was in tears i replied really no cancer, she said yes my darling you are going to be fine and said we will still need you to come back up to the hospital on the 12th so we can take out your last drainage pipe at 12.45 and said we will see you then, i replied thankyou with tears still rolling down my face. I put the phone down hubby was by the side of me on the bed when i got the call; we just looked at each other and cuddled and cried together. I phoned my daughter and told her the news she was so happy i then told my two boys and the rest of my family, it was good news all round. I phoned my best mate to tell the news and she was so happy she replied thank god i couldn't have lived my life without you, you could hear in her voice she was crying. We were really close as we had gone to school together and she was the one that had saved my life that day i took my overdose. Her life was not going to great for her as she had broken her leg and was starting to get depressed, she also suffered with anxiety we just got closer and closer everyday we spent together we started to become like sisters. She was not just an old school friend she was my best mate and i was hers, we seemed to have both gone downhill together but we knew no matter what we were there for each other. She had lost her dog shadow not long after i had lost dibbles and what seemed to be happening to me was also happening to her, i loved that girl with all my heart. It reminded me a lot of my mum and the best friend that she had, they had grown up together and to this day 22years after mum had died she still goes to my mum's grave stone and place's flowers, she has never forgot my mum and to me that is what you call a true friend, where not even the death of my mum took away the friendship they had. It took a while for my news to sink in as my anxiety had got so bad with all the worry of not knowing it just continued to stay at that level for a very long time which did shock me as i thought it would have calmed down but that just wasn't the case. I went to my appointment at the hospital on the 12th to have my last drainage pipe taken out and my bandages taken off, i was shocked to see that after only nine days my scares were not that noticeable i was reminded that my results were all clear. I was told to come back in three months time so they could check on my progress, my auntie had come along with me and hubby to the hospital to give us some support and i wanted to say a big thankyou to her for that as she had supported me throughout my ordeal from the very start when i was first diagnosed with the radial scar right to the end. If i am honest i don't think i could got through it without her, she will never know how much it meant to me her helping me through my terrible ordeal and how much i have grown to love her. I also wanted to thank my dad, my older brother and his wife for the support they all gave to me on the night of my operation. My dad was there when i needed him the most sometimes i never really felt my dad loved me but that night the look in his eyes was a look of love, so thank you for being there that night and for the support after i came home to dad. As for my older brother we had not really been in each others lifes much after mum had died and for him show up at the hospital that night alongside his wife just to be there for me when we had not seen each other for so long meant the world to me, he showed his love for me that day and i will never forget that for as long as i live. He continued to support me after my operation with day to day phone calls just to see how i was, i just wanted to say thankyou to the both of you and that i love you for all the support you gave me when i needed it the most. As time went by after getting my results i started to feel better in myself after the operation but my anxiety was still out of control and could only be managed with my medication. Hubby was going deeper into depression he was still taking his medication but it wasn't helping him much as he was still smoking cannabis alongside the medication and we all know cannabis is an anti-depressant in itself, he was aware of this but didn't know how else to deal with his emotions, he felt no reason to get up in the mornings and he was so angry all the time. He felt like he just couldn't cope with life anymore, i tried to understand him the best i could as i had anxiety and depression to but for me my tablets were helping me cope with mine, the tablets did their part but the rest was down to me but because hubby was smoking cannabis his tablets were not working. He first started using cannabis to help him sleep as he just couldn't sleep at night, sometimes he wouldn't get to sleep until 3 am and sometimes not sleep at all. As time went by he started using more and more of the cannabis in the day time to help him deal with his anxiety and it was starting to cost him more and more, he never ever touched the money we got to live on as he still had a little of his savings from when he lost his job. He had already tried hard a few times to give up the cannabis but i noticed with him trying to cope without it any little thing would make him feel angry and found himself going back to it, just when things couldn't get any worse for us we received a letter from the council saying that they had reduced our housing benefit as our son was working and because he was 18 years old he had to contribute towards the rent. We had to hand in three of his wage slips as the council had it down that he was earning £380 pounds a week and he only had a job at fast food restaurant, the most he would earn was £150 a week so until we handed in the wage slips they would not be willing to start paying the full rent until they had checked it all out, So with that we had to make up the difference in the rent which put more pressure on us both that we really didn't need. We couldn't cope with anymore bad luck so the next day we went down to the council and handed in our son's wage slips, we were told it would take a while for them to sort it all out. I felt sick to the stomach all this so soon after i was told i didn't have cancer, i was in so much pain still with my breast but i can honestly say i have lived and learned, believe me when i tell you i have learned that life can treat you so cruel with no answers to why. Words are beyond me now we just keep getting so much bad luck time after time we were finding it so hard to stay positive, I am 38 years old and all i have ever wanted is my mum. Ever since my radial scar i haven't been able to get my mum out of my mind, i spend everyday fighting so hard to keep it all together so why do i feel that just because i suffer with depression i feel like i have done something wrong. So many people look at you differently, all they tell you is that they don't understand and you need to snap yourself out of it. I didn't choose depression depression chose me and if it was as easy as some people think it is just to snap your self out of it then nobody in this world would have depression, if only it was that easy. Depression is a mental illness and so many people choose to ignore that, my saying has always been unless you have ever suffered with depression yourself you will never understand how hard life can be for you and how lonely life can be. I get very angry at times because unless you've walked that path of having to deal with depression then you have no right to judge anybody who has a mental health problem. My best mate was 17weeeks pregnant and we had been talking over the phone for the last few days as she had been in a lot of pain over the weekend. I had been worried about her as we always talked on the phone and if we didn't talk by phone then we would text each other everyday to see how each other was getting on. On the 5th of December she had been telling me that she was in alot of pain and that she didn't get any sleep the night before, she had to be up the hospital for 10 o' clock to have a scan on Monday to check that her baby was ok, i told to her phone me and let me know how she got on and she replied i will. The following morning she had her scan at 10 o' clock, i remember i had alot to do that day as me and hubby had to go into town to get our grandsons birthday presents, it got to about 9.30

that Monday night and i still hadn't heard from her so i sent her a text and said hi sis how are you and how did the scan go, it took a while before i received a text back but when i did it said things ain't good sis i am back in hospital. I went straight into panic mode as it wasn't like her not to ring or text so i knew something had to be wrong, i phoned her home to speak to her partner and her mum picked the phone up and told me why she was in hospital. Her mum explained to me that Lynn had delivered her baby at home and that the baby had passed away, i was in complete shock i couldn't believe what her mum had just told me, once i had put the phone down i couldn't hold back my emotions i was in bits i couldn't believe what she had gone through. Oh god i kept saying not Lynn i got a text come through from her saying she had lost her baby, we were sending such sad text messages to each other, i could tell she was crying in her texts i was to. I got a text from her saying the doctor had just been in to tell her she had a baby boy, i felt so helpless that i couldn't be with her it felt like my heart had been ripped out again. The text messages stopped coming as it was now early hours of the morning, i won't explain what my sis had to go through as it is to distressing to put in to words what she had to deal with at home when she lost her baby that day. She still to this day finds it so hard to talk about, we spoke on the phone once she was back home and it was so painful for her to explain to me what had happened. I listened to her cries and felt her pain i felt helpless as i could not do anything to help her apart from support her through her terrible pain. She had a service for her baby boy who they named junior, on the 17th December and rest in peace little man junior i dedicated my own poem to my sis and her partner in memory of their baby boy junior.

A silent tear we wipe away, As we recall that December day, No time to say goodbye, Heartaches in this world are many, but losing you junior was greater than any, Forgive us if we should weep, For our son we loved but could not keep, Today tomorrow our whole life through, We will never get over losing you, No one knew what that day would bring, For your precious heart stopped beating, And we could not do a thing, Whatever else we fail to do, We never fail to think of you, Deep in our hearts, Your memories kept, When we come to see you we place your flowers with care, But no one knows the heartache we bear, As we turn and leave you there, With tears in our eyes we whisper low, God bless you baby junior, We love you so, In loving memory of baby junior may he rest in peace.

My sis and her partner continued to grieve after the loss of their baby boy junior for many months and sadly all i could do was be there for her throughout her loss. I went to see sis on the 20th as we hadn't seen each other since she had lost junior, she showed me a picture of him and he was so gorgeous he really was, i know she will never get over this but time is a healer and i just hope and pray she will get through this. Always thinking of you sis and love you with all my heart. We celebrated our grandsons 2nd birthday on the 8th December, bless him he has brought so much happiness to our lifes but it's been hard to be able to enjoy him as much as we would have liked to, as i have had depression for so long in his young life and all the problems along the way with hubby suffering with depression also and me being in and out of hospital, then the radial scar. It has been hard but he knows how much we love him and in a way it's a blessing that he is too young to understand. I did think a lot about my sis on our grandson's birthday as she only lost junior the day before so my heart was with her also. It wasn't long before mine and hubby's depression got worse as we were getting letters coming through the door about all our debts, we were paying a £100 a month out of what little money we had and could no longer afford the payments anymore. The council were also saying we owed £450 and we just didn't know which way to turn, hubby still had a drug habit and carried alot of guilt with it, some people may say well give it up and you would have some money but it had gone too far for that as he was also having alot of suicidal thoughts as Christmas day he felt the time was right to get answers off of his mum about his past to do with his childhood. He was really angry on that day as he had lived with this since he was 9 years old and it came to a head that day, he phoned his mum and asked her all he wanted to know. In the back of his mind he didn't think that his mum would tell him the truth about his dad and why she had put him through what she did, but to his shock she did and it ended up being a very emotional phone call for the both of them. Once he had come of the phone he seemed to feel better for it until a few days later when it hit him hard as he was told the real reason why his dad had committed suicide, it was the for same reason hubby found himself in, where he didn't have a job, he had depression and was in debt and couldn't pay the bills. His dad did what he did because he had life insurance and with being told this hubby didn't know how to cope or deal with the answers he was given from his mum about his dad. We had our daughter, her partner and our grandson down for Christmas afternoon and it ended being a nice day especially after the Christmas we had last year. After we got Christmas out the way things just turned from bad to worse as the letters kept coming, we were told if we didn't pay the rent arrears on the house then we were not entitled to the house so we were under alot of pressure and that was sending us deeper and deeper into depression. We were both having suicidal thoughts and it was just getting out of control. I had found two more lumps on my left breast and I was already told i had to have yearly checks as the radial scar could appear in my other breast, so i had to go back to the hospital for a ultra sound which sent my alarm bells ringing but things where ok as it showed up on the scan that it was actually my implant, the implant had a lump on each corner so they could check the implant was in the right position so that was one less thing we had to worry about. After Christmas and new year was out of the way i was just hoping and praying that this year was going to be a bit easier than last year, i knew we still had alot to deal with but after my radial scar i just couldn't bair anymore bad luck as we had already had more than our fair share of bad luck. I still had my appointment at the hospital on February 2nd to have more surgery on my rebuild so i knew that last year would follow into this year, we still had all our debts to deal with so we weren't holding out too much hope. We were already in the start of January and my depression and anxiety was still very bad. Hubby wasn't getting any better if anything he seemed to be getting worse as we always spoke to each other about how we felt, we just found that when we took a step back and looked at our lifes hubby was going through what his dad did, and i was going through what mum did and hand on heart to know we were both feeling like we were living the lives our parents did our life was not a good place to be. How could our lifes have gone so terribly wrong, we had ten years of not a great life but we had self respect as we were working, we could hold our heads up high as we were providing for our family. We had our ups and downs in life like everyone does, i still had my days where i would get low about mum but it never sent me into depression. I found living and coping with my I.B.S was always hard to live with but i had had it for so many years now i had forgotten what it was like to be normal, and again unless you are an I.B.S sufferer you would never understand what it's like to live with this on a day to day basis, when you have had it for as long as i have you have to accept it's part of your life now. I remember my mate had it for a week and she couldn't cope with it, she had said to me she didn't know how i had coped with it for the last 15 years, i would have days where i was ill with my I.B.S, i use to think about cancer but put every illness i had down to the I.B.S. I had always had a fear of cancer and was scared that one day i might get cancer, but i became a positive person in those ten years and maybe that's what got me through it.

Ever since i was told i had radial scar and had to have my breast removed with the not knowing if i had cancer or not, those ten days of waiting for my results i had to face my fear of cancer and i wasn't scared of it anymore, even when i found out i didn't have cancer i felt after time i was more scared of the depression, anxiety and panic attacks than cancer, because with depression you don't feel in control of your life anymore, sometimes i would have days were i would feel in control of my life and other days the anxiety and depression would take back that control and for me it felt like mental torture especially when i would get suicidal thoughts with it. It's a really scary feeling because not only would i be fighting the depression and anxiety, the suicidal thoughts were much more powerful and with hubby feeling the same to i had lost my rock. We had to learn to deal with it in our own way, sometimes we were like to snakes in a cage we only had each other to take it out on. I had my support from my case worker and was also having weekly sessions of C.B.T which seemed to be helping me now but hubby only had the support of his doctor at st clements. With his drug habit getting out of control the more he was smoking the more he hated himself for it but for me i would much rather him find his own way of coping with the depression and anxiety, aswell as all the suicidal thoughts what he was smoking wasn't an issue for me, keeping him safe was my number one priority as we had already been through so much torment. He was beating himself up so bad with all the guilt of smoking cannabis because we were in so much debt, he even found it hard to look at himself in the mirror he hated himself that much. I didn't like him smoking it but i had to look past that and take into account the reason why he was smoking it. I knew it wasn't making him any better but for me it was keeping him stable and most importantly it was keeping him safe. I fell ill again as i ended up getting another urine infection so i felt low in myself again, my hospital appointment wasn't until the 5th of March to dicuss the surgery. We were getting phone calls aswell as letters coming through the door about our debts; it was just getting to the point where we couldn't deal with living like this anymore. Mine and hubby's depression was getting so bad we were beginning to start talking about acting on our suicidal thoughts, we went as far as phoning the council up and asking them if anything happened to us would the house go to our boy's, they replied yes and with that we had alot of disturbing thoughts just thinking if we committed suicide our debts would be wiped and the boys would have a roof over their heads. I had to see my case worker the following morning and she advised us to go to C.A.B to see if we could get help with our debts, so we went down and saw a financial advisor and we spoke about what we owed, he advised us that the only option we really had was to go bankrupt as we couldn't even afford to make token payments as we were only living on my E.S.A. He told us he would phone our creditors up on our behalf and talk to them about putting our debts on hold for 30 days and that he would phone us within a few days, so with that we felt a bit more at ease. I still felt really ill as my urine infection had gone to my kidneys again so i was laid up in bed for most of that week, i was getting worried because my hospital appointment was coming up soon and i wasn't sure if a date would be set for me to have my surgery. I just felt like everything that could go wrong was going wrong, i was at my wits end. I know life is hard but this was starting to get unbearable for me and hubby, we weren't sleeping as we still hadn't heard anything back from C.A.B. The phone calls were coming in the daytime aswell as at night the threatening letters were still coming on a daily basis, we still had the council on our back wanting us to pay what we owed. I then got called in for an appointment down the social to do with my E,S,A as i had to have a medical assessment to see if i was still entitled to the benefit i was getting, i took my case worker along with me for some support as she was aware of my mental state which was getting worse, i was asked a lot of questions by the women doing the interview and as we got towards the end of my interview she ask me to stand up to do some arm movements, i did my left arm but i could only get my right arm up half way as i was still in alot of pain with my scar where i had my internal bleed, so when i go to stretch my arm up my scar gets so tight it becomes very uncomfortable and painful, so with that the women said to me ok that's fine. She then asked me if i could loosen my clothing on my top half so that she could see proof of the scar, with no time to think i loosened my top and showed her my scar. She then said ok thankyou that's about it you should get a phone call to let you know the outcome of our decision, with that me and my case worker walked out, i said to my case worker as we were walking out how can she do that ask to see proof of my scar when she had all my hospital letters and the doctors reports of what i have been through. My case worker replied i know i was very shocked by that to and if i wanted she would put in a complaint, i replied yes please. Days went by and i just found myself in disbelief that i had to show her proof that i had a scar in that interview. I felt emotionally sick to my stomach, i kept saying to myself that she must have thought that i was making up the whole thing; i was in complete shock and felt mental disturbed by this. I thought if this is how women get treated after having their breast removed something is not right they shouldn't be allowed to do that. My mind went back to thinking about mum when she had her breast removed they never did rebuilds back in 1989 so all my poor mum did have was just the scars, i will never forget as long as i live when i was at home that day, dad was back at work and mum told me she was going to have a bath and i replied ok mum. I was downstairs and i heard my mum scream out in tears, i went running up to the bathroom and said to mum are you ok, but mum just told me to go away nobody would want me looking like this, i was 15 years old at the time and to this day i still have nightmares of my mum screaming. I just can't put into words how that woman has made me feel, i was just sinking deeper into depression, my I.B.S was getting really bad as the more stress i was under the worse it would get, it's a known fact that stress causes I.B.S to flair up. A week had gone by and i had a phone call in the afternoon from a guy to tell me that i had lost my E.S.A and that i wouldn't be getting any more payments, he said i could put in for an appeal against their decision so i was in complete shock, he then said is there anything else i can do to help i replied no thanks and ended the call. I just sat on my bed and cried and told myself no more i can't cope with life being this bad, i felt i had reached my point of no return i was running suicidal thoughts through my head of how to end my life without hurting my children. I was getting scared as i felt i had no control over my life anymore, it started off my panic attacks and i had the scariest panic attack i have ever experienced it lasted for hours, even with two of my tablets that i had taken to try and calm me down i was just going out of my mind. After a while the tablets kicked in and i started to put things in to perspective and told myself i can do this and no matter what i am not going to let my depression take me away from my children because my children are my life and they all still needed me. I had to start fighting back, life can knock us down but it's whether we choose to get back up and i was determined that whatever life threw at me i was not going down. I had come through too much to give up on myself now, i was smoking more and more and i had never smoked in my life up until 2 years ago, it was just my way of coping but i hated smoking it just wasn't me and the more i tried to get through this the harder life seemed to be getting, i feel i haven't had a chance to deal with my radial scar before me and hubby got hit with another problem. I just feel like I'm in a big hole and someone has just buried me alive, but where there's a will there's got to be a way and i just have to hold on to that with both hands, no matter how much i long to be with mum again i believe i didn't get cancer for a reason and one day that will become clear. Suicidal thoughts are powerful but with depression you have to find your inner strength to overpower those thoughts, so even though i think about suicide putting those thoughts in to action takes a lot of guts to act on those thoughts. I couldn't put my kids through losing their mum, i know the pain i have had to live with without my mum in my life and i wouldn't wish that on my kids. They have supported me and their dad throughout our depression and helped us the best way that they can. We have three great kids and we share all our feelings as a family, we've always been there for one another and as long as we have each other we can get through anything. I saw my case worker the next day and told her how i felt and she replied you can do this i know you can, i know things are hard but i have faith in you that you will get through this. She told me she was going to put us forward to a charity that support people that are having money problems, she was also going to put in an appeal against the decision on my E,S,A. I always felt better with the support of my case worker as she would try her best to help me carry the load so that my mental state didn't deteriorate, a week went by and we got a phone call off of a women from the charity and she said that she would come round to ours on Tuesday January 25th to assess what help we needed so we only had a few days to wait. We had little food in the house and i only had £20 left in my purse but we managed to get through the next two days, we had our meeting with the women from the charity and she was very helpful she told us she would get in touch with welfare rights and see if she could get us some tokens for food, she also said she would get in touch with the council on our behalf to find out how we managed to owe this £450 rent on our house when we were in credit with our rent before they started paying housing benefit. She was in disbelief that we had gone to C.A.B and hadn't even heard back from them, she advised us to go back down to C.A.B to speak to the guy we had spoken to and find out if anything had been done. Hubby contacted C.A.B to find out what had been done only to find out the guy we had spoke to wasn't due back until March, so hubby asked if any action had been taken in regards to our case and was told that no steps had been taken yet. So hubby went mad, he asked them if he could come and collect all our documents so we could seek advice elsewhere only to be told they didn't know where the financial advisor had put our file and they were unsure whether it was actually in his office or whether he had taken it home. They were unable to gain access to his office to check as it was locked and he had the only key, so we were completely stuffed. We spoke to the lady from the charity to see what we could do and what alternative options we had, she advised us to seek financial advice from another organisation and offered to put us in contact with a charity organisation that dealt with financial situations like ours. In the mean time we had to apply for a crisis loan as i had still not heard anything back about my E.S.A. We were in complete dismay as all they would give us to live on was £94 but was told to phone back the following week if i still hadn't heard anything about my E.S.A. With this hubby was getting more and more angry, he felt the system was letting us down as he had paid £7500 to the tax man in January, The system was supposed to be there for people to help them, where had our help been ever since hubby was made redundant, it seemed as though they just didn't want to know, they take your money whilst your earning but won't give anything back when you lose your job. This was pushing hubby deeper and deeper into depression, he wanted so bad just to be back at work and providing for his family. Everything he had worked for he had to sell to keep food on the table and to cover the cost of his cannabis addiction as smoking the cannabis was the only way he felt he could cope with everything that was happening and to keep his aggression under control, he was getting so angry with the way we had been let down. We were still receiving the daily phone calls and letters from the debt collectors. We got a phone call from the woman from the charity, she told us she had managed to get us a little bit of help, she had managed to get us food tokens for the sum of £50 a week but this would only be for six weeks, we were grateful for the smallest amount of help. We had to sit the boys down and explain to them the seriousness of our situation and there was a chance that we may lose our home, We also explained to them that we may have to go bankrupt as we couldn't afford to pay the creditors and because of the medication we were on and what we were dealing with we were not mentally stable enough to go back to work. Whilst i was waiting to hear about my E.S.A hubby rang to see if he could re-claim job seekers allowance, he explained to the advisor over the phone that he was on medication for anxiety and depression. He was told he wasn't eligible to claim job seekers as he wasn't fit for work and was advised to claim for E.S.A the same as me, so with that he went to make a claim for E.S.A only to be told they couldn't process a claim for him as i was appealing against their decision on my E.S.A and that really wound him up he started shouting at them down the phone about the way they had dealt with us and they just put the phone down. The following week we had to phone again for a crisis loan but was refused as they said it showed on their system my E.S.A had been reinstated and i would be receiving a payment the following day which was a bit of good luck at last. I had to go back up to the hospital on the 31st January to sign my consent forms ready for the surgery on my bladder. I had just got to wait now as i hadn't been given a date as to when my surgery would be, but fingers crossed it would not be too much longer as i was still continually getting urine infections. That was getting me down a lot to as it was hard to go anywhere when i felt the need to pass urine every five minutes. I went back up the hospital again on the 2nd of February for my appointment to do with my breast and i was seen by a different surgeon, as the surgeon who had done my operation last year had left Ipswich hospital to go to west Suffolk hospital in Bury st Edmunds. I felt a little disappointed as i had put my trust in that surgeon because she had done my surgery and saved my life when i had the internal bleed, I was told by the surgeon that was now taking her place that she would not be willing to do anymore surgery on my breast until later on in the year as i was still very badly bruised and that if she did anymore surgery now it could lead to me having further complications. I was told to come back in June so she could check that my breast had healed properly and she would take things from there. I was glad in a way that i was not going to have anymore surgery just yet as i didn't feel mentally stable enough to go for more surgery. I was already still waiting to have surgery on my bladder which i had to face so maybe it was a good thing. I wasn't happy with the way my breast looked but i could get past that as i just thought about mum and her not having any breast there at all, it made me be thankful that i had the chance to have my breast rebuilt on the same day of my surgery. I find myself thinking that i wished me and hubby didn't have so much to cope with so soon after my radial scar as i do believe i would of had time to come to terms with what had happened to me, i would of found it easier to deal with but because we had so much going on i feel i haven't had the chance to accept that part of my life yet. As weeks went by me and hubby just tried to hold it together as much as possible, it was as hard as it was when i lost mum. My world felt so empty and everyday i would just write in a day to day diary about how much i was missing her and still after 22 long years i still can't believe mum has gone, she was so young when she died and all she had the chance to do with her life was have us kids. When a person like my nana and granddad who had lived a full life passes away it didn't stop the pain i went through after losing nana two years ago, but there is sense that everything is as it should be, but when someone dies young like my mum did there's a sadness that goes beyond normal the same as with babies like little junior as there seems no justification for it, i think once we are connected to our loved ones it doesn't make sense that the connection we had with our loved ones should be broken just because they are not with us anymore, i believe our connection should never broken as long as we exist the connection with our love ones stays. I have always wanted to write a book in memory of my mum for the last 22 years but never thought i would ever do it until what happened to me with my radial scar, being the same age as mum i decided the time was right for me to put pen to paper and grant myself that wish of writing my own book about my life without my mum. I know i am not the only one that has loved and lost their mum, we all have at some point in our lifes lost somebody we loved, but for me i wanted the world to know that my mum had left behind an amazing legacy, not only as an amazing mother but for the person she was because before she become a mum she was a person, a person that would be there for anyone, she had a gifted heart and it is a true saying that god only takes the best, just a bit too soon though. I received a phone call from the hospital on the 24th of February to say that they had a space the next day at 7.30 in the morning for the surgery on my bladder, i started to feel my anxiety well up knowing i had got more surgery in the morning, my auntie was at mine the day i got the call and she gave me a lot of support, telling me that i would be ok. My auntie has always given me great support; we didn't really have much to do with each other up to the point when nana fell ill. When i got depression she was there for me, i found her so easy to talk to as she would never judge me for anything and we would talk about her and mum when they were little girls, she supported me through my radial scar, it was so hard for my auntie as she had lost her mum her dad and her sister had died so young, now her family had gone she found that so hard. Then she had to watch me go through what mum did and she was my rock, she feels more like a mum now than my auntie and when i think about it i was supposed to be the one that looked after her for my nana, but there she was looking after me and being my support. I just wish i would have got to know her sooner because i could have loved her for longer. Me and hubby got up early as we had to be at the hospital for 7.30 my anxiety was bad, just the thought of going back into surgery so soon after my last operation as it had only been three and a half months and my operation went so wrong, i was feeling scared to go back but i needed to have it done as i just couldn't cope with all the urine infections i kept on having, when we got to the hospital i was seen by the surgeon and he explained what he would be doing and said i should be going up to theatre around about 8.30. My anxiety was so bad i couldn't control it so i had to take a tablet to calm it down, with that they were ready for me i asked if it was ok for hubby to walk down with us to the theatre room, so they let hubby come until we got into the theatre, hubby kissed me goodbye and then left. I started to have a panic attack and the surgeon asked if i was ok, i replied can you just put me to sleep with tears rolling down my face and with that i slowly differed of to sleep. I woke up in the recovery room and saw the lights on the ceiling, it brought back memories of my last operation and i just wanted to get out, i couldn't bair to lay there remembering the flash backs of my last operation. It wasn't long before i was back up on the ward and when i saw hubby it felt like heaven, with a sigh of relief it was one operation down and just one more to go. I was sent home soon after my operation and just laid in bed for the rest of the day. The next day i felt really empty i kept asking myself should i have gone for that operation i don't think i was mentally stable enough to go through another operation. I still hadn't dealt with my last operation i just wanted all the torment to stop, as a long side all the bad luck we kept on getting my depression was getting worse. I felt everytime i saw someone i had to put on a front and pretend that i was ok but in reality all i was doing was hiding behind a fake smile because inside i felt so sad as me hubby still had so much to cope with, i personally couldn't see any light at the end of the tunnel. My case worker came to see me the day after my operation and she said to me that i would get through this. She had been my case worker for two years and she told me she had seen the fight in me, and that even though i didn't feel strong at the moment she had every faith in me that she would see that fight in me again. People do have their own beliefs that medication does more harm than good with depression, but for me i wouldn't be here today without it and i would go as far as saying it did save my life. Depression is such a hard mental illness to deal with, one day you can have a good day and the next you can have the worst day ever, i was just glad that this operation was over and done with. Hubby's depression was still out of control and he was still using the cannabis to help cope with his depression, with my depression i was still at my wits end as my anxiety was getting worse, we both still continued to have suicidal thoughts and still found ourselves talking about just ending our lifes, which for us was so hard as the suicidal thoughts were getting more and more powerful, the more powerful they got for us both the less control we felt we had over our lifes. We had so many debts to contend with we just couldn't see any way out, we still had our weekly visits from the women that was trying to help us sort out our debts and the issue we had with the council over the rent, she also came round to give us £50 a week to help us to live on she was doing her best to get as much help and support us as she could. This didn't leave me hubby with any dignity as we felt we had to beg for food just to get us by. I had been with hubby for 18 years and i had only ever seen him cry a few times but since he had been suffering with depression i was seeing him cry on a daily basis and that killed me, i just wanted to wave a magic wand and make it all go away for him i couldn't bair to see him cry, i felt so helpless i would walk away from him and go into a different room and cry myself but i had to try and be strong for him when i saw him so upset. Seeing someone you love so much and hearing them say that they don't even know who they are anymore is so soul destroying. Hubby found it so hard to deal with that he had become so dependent on the cannabis, he hated himself so much and no matter what i tried to say or do to make him feel better about himself it was how he felt as a person inside and nobody could change the way he felt, he felt as though he was a complete failure to me his children, his grandson but most of all to himself that he couldn't support his family anymore. He would just repeatedly say with tears rolling down his face i can't live like this anymore, so at times i had to be strong and tell him i don't know how but we will get through this we have to for our children. Hubby had put all what he had into trying to give up the cannabis but the harder he would try and fail the less of a man he felt, i was so scared that when i was asleep if hubby had a really bad day that he would try and harm himself, because i would go off to sleep about 12 midnight and he would still be awake till early hours of the morning, so i just had to put my trust in him that he wouldn't do anything stupid. Today is the 31st of March the day mum died 22 years ago and also the day me and hubby got married, it was hubby's birthday to. This day was always hard for me but this year it was even harder as life for my family was hard, the day of hubbys birthday he stayed in our bedroom because he just couldn't deal with having a birthday, our daughter came to see him with our grandson and he would just put on a front for the sake of our grandson so he didn't pick up on anything, our daughter knew her dad wasn't right so she had a talk to him and it was so hard for her to see me and her dad so depressed but she understood as she had suffered with depression herself once before and knew how hard it was. The day of hubby's birthday he finally showed her his emotions and cried to her saying how he felt and she sat and listened and tried to support her dad the best she could. It was hard on our daughter as she was the oldest out of the three so she understood more why me and her dad felt the way we did as she had her own house and it's a worry when you can't pay your bills, our daughter loved her dad no matter what, she would never hear a bad word said about him or me she just took us both under her wing and tried to be there for us both as much as possible. Our youngest son has a girlfriend and her mum has bipolar and she suffers with depression, anxiety and panic attacks aswell. His girlfriend had been through so much and our son knows what we have been through, he has been a great support to his girlfriend and her mum, once his girlfriends mum was having a panic attack at her home when our son was there and he knew how to handle the situation, he knew how to calm her mum down and to tell her to breath he was great. I wanted to try and explain depression and anxiety to people for them to try and get a better picture of how a person feels to live with depression and anxiety on a daily basis, it's not to get people to help us in any way or feel sorry for us, it's just to try and get people to understand us better and how hard it is to live with. Most of the time negative emotions don't come in pure packages. In fact anxiety and depression usually go hand in hand, however the feelings are very different from each other anxiety results from the perception of danger. You can feel anxious if you think to yourself that something terrible is about to happen. For example if you have a fear of heights and you're hiking on a mountain trail with steep drop-offs you'll probably feel gripped by panic because you'll think that you could slip and fall at any moment. In contrast when you're depressed you feel like the tragedy has already happened, it seems like you've already fallen off the cliff and you're lying at the bottom of a ravine broken beyond repair with no escape. You feel blue, demoralized and down in the dumps, You tell yourself that you're worthless and that you're a failure, or that you're not nearly as good as you should be. You lose interest in life and in other people; the activities you once enjoyed seem unrewarding and nothing excites you anymore. You feel overwhelmed and life seems like one long journey. The worst part is the hopelessness you feel, like things will never change and you believe that you'll be miserable forever; you think that other people are looking down on you or thinking that you are weird, if only they knew how you really felt inside. I hope this helps people to understand how depression makes a person feel about themselves and once again nobody chooses depression depression chooses them. So many people have committed suicide because they feel they have no support and that people don't want to understand what they are going through, for me and hubby we only have the support of those who have suffered with depression and it makes me feel sad and very lonely because for me i don't want to be looked at as weird or abnormal to anybody. At the end of the day i am still me under the depression and really loving someone is to look past that. Hubby and i fight our depression everyday and it is not easy but we fight for our children and our grandson. Nobody knows how we feel behind closed doors only we do and all I can say is i am thankful i had those ten years of my life where i was free from depression, for me now though after suffering again for 2 years with depression its like those ten years never existed. I still have weekly visits from my case worker and the woman helping us with our debts we had some support with our money worries. On April 12th hubby decided that he was going to give up the cannabis and for the first day he was doing really well, it was going to be hard for him as he had never dealt with his depression without the cannabis, he would have to deal with the withdrawals of coming off the cannabis as well, he had done one whole day and didn't even think about it and i was so proud of him, he had done so well i didn't know if hubby could do it as he had tried so many times in the past all i could do was tell him if you know in yourself this isn't for you anymore then you can do this. Day's went by then weeks and finally one month had past and still no cannabis, hubby started to feel he had a little bit more control in his life now he was starting to deal with his addiction to cannabis. It was great news that hubby had his cannabis addiction under control but he was finding his depression hard to cope with, he would have so many bad days where he would get really low but didn't return back to his cannabis addiction, our children were so proud of him and for me i felt more proud for him because he hated himself so much and had carried alot of guilt because of his cannabis addiction, so for him to be able to look at himself now he felt a lot better that he was back in control and that he no longer depended on the cannabis. Depression is so hard to beat we would both have days where we didn't even want to see anyone, we didn't feel like eating and hubby had lost 3 stone which was a worry because he started to look ill but he just found it so hard to eat anything big. He is just getting by eating tiny amounts of food like crackers and yoghurt; he still can't handle anything like a cooked roast dinner as he would be in so much pain with his tummy. We had a meeting with the guy who was sorting out for me hubby to go bankrupt he told us that it was going to be a bit of a challenge for him to try and get help from a charity as he had never applied for a couple before as it was a lot of money to claim for it was £450 each to go bankrupt plus £150 each for court costs so in total he had to try to get £1200 which is a lot of money, we were also told that our banks would get shut down, we also had to fill in some paperwork. it was hard not to walk away and not worry as we still had letters everyday and the phone calls but to top it all off we had already had one visit from the bailiffs, so we felt we were under alot of pressure thinking if we didn't get the help from the charity to go bankrupt we didn't know what we were going to do. We still had the council sending letters demanding their money so we felt like we had it coming from all angles, we couldn't sleep we were worrying ourselves to the point where our depression was getting out of control even with the medication we were on. Hubby and i was having weekly visits with our doctors up st clements as we were both experiencing suicidal thoughts again, so we had to be monitored weekly for that. Hubby started having alot of panic attacks due to all the pressure and the worry of not knowing which way to turn we had so much to cope with, with all problems we had to sort out before we had the chance to deal with one situation another one would arise, we were just going out of our mind we had so much to deal with but it was just sending us deeper and deeper into depression. We would try and get out of the house just to give us room to think, there had to be a better way to deal with what we were going through as we were both feeling worried, nervous, afraid and angry that we had such little control over our lifes. We felt that nothing was getting any better we were in such a dark place and every new day that came we hoped would be better but that was never the case, we were struggling just trying to get through the day dealing with the depression and anxiety. Everything seemed to be spiralling out of control and we felt so alone, we just wanted to give up the will to live this wasn't a life it was hell. My birthday was on May 13th i was now 39 years old the same age my mum was when she died, i felt in disbelief that for me i had reached my mums age now and after going through losing my breast and going back to November not knowing if i had cancer or not was the worst days of my life, i really thought that i was going to die to the point where i had even wrote my own children a poem to read after i was gone. It was almost as if i was preparing myself to die this has had a massive impact on my mental state, people can judge you and say just get over it you didn't have cancer but that gets me very angry it wasn't the case that i didn't have cancer it was the mental torture of going through the whole experience which isn't as easy as one might think. Everyday i look at my scar and it's a constant reminder of that experience. I have come to terms with what has happened to me i just don't know how to cope or deal with it. I still don't have the full use my right arm and when i do simple things like housework, painting, gardening, i get a constant throbbing pain in my breast, pins needles in my hands and numbness in my arm, it's very hard for me to explain how this makes me feel to people who have not gone through the same experience, it's how it makes you feel as a person inside i wish i could just forget and move on from this but how can you move on from something when it's not over with. I still have to have one more operation to rebuild my breast properly and it scares me so much because my first operation went so horribly wrong. So if i decide not to have the surgery and just live with my breast the way it is at the moment is something i don't think i can do. Or do i have more surgery to make me feel better as a woman and take the risk of losing what i have or the risk that something may go wrong again is hard decision to make. I then have to deal with the mixed emotions i have about mum and how she must have felt having to lose her breast completely and not having the option of a rebuild. I have alot of mixed emotions where my mum is concerned and find it hard to separate them both. Sometimes i look at what my mum had to go through 22 years ago and what she had to deal with as she was actually diagnosed with cancer, so she had to go through all the chemotherapy and the fear she may lose her hair, i feel so selfish sometimes as i was lucky to the extent that mine wasn't cancerous, yes i had to lose my breast but my mum lost her life. So how do i decide what is the best thing for me to do. I know i have to make this decision for myself but what is the best decision all round, do i take a chance of having more surgery and risk putting my family through more heartache or do i deal with what i have and put myself through the heartache of never being happy ever again and not being able to look at myself in a mirror without having the constant reminder that i will never feel like a complete woman again. We got a phone call a few weeks later from the guy who was trying to get us the financial help to enable us to go bankrupt, luckily enough it was good news he had managed to get the full amount through a charity to enable us to both go bankrupt. We had to go into his office to fill out the bankruptcy forms and sign for the cheques, we were given the dates that we had to attend court and hubby's couldn't of fallen on a worse day, his day in court was the 25th of may the day my nana had died and mine was the following day on the 26th. Even though going bankrupt took the financial pressure off of us it didn't make us feel any better, it actually made hubby more depressed as he felt so angry, he felt as though we had been forced into bankruptcy because if the system would of helped him when he needed it most we would never have been put in the position where we had no choice but to go bankrupt. My younger sister Rebecca got married on the 21st of May to her partner, she looked stunning on her wedding day and even though she had always looked at me as a motherly figure i know deep in her heart she wished our mum could have been there. It was a day of mixed emotions for me i had tears of joy because i was there to watch her get married and know that she now had her own family to care for, the motherly instincts i had for her had always been there from the first day i started taking care of them and i think in a way they always will be. I also had tears of pain as i thought of my mum and what she had missed out on as she should have been there to watch her youngest daughter get married and start a life of her own. At her reception she was given a wedding present from my aunt, none of us could of imagined it but it was a beautifully framed picture of my mum, it brought us all to tears as Rebecca gave it a place of pride, she placed it on the main table in front of her wedding cake for everyone to see. Having the photo there was as though mum was there watching over her on her special day. Half way through the evening my dad decided to make a speech and to all our shock he brought mum into his speech but you could tell it came from the heart, it had the whole family in tears my brothers, sisters, aunt's, uncles and cousins. My sister and now husband left the reception early as they had to get home as they were off on their honeymoon and were leaving in the early hours of the morning. It was a day i would treasure for the rest of my life. Even though my younger siblings were all now grown up with families and lives of their own, deep in my heart they will always in some way still feel like my children and in theirs they will always know that no matter what i will always be there for them with open arms. The night before hubby was due in court for his bankruptcy our anxiety and depression was way out of control, we both sat there thinking whether we were doing the right thing going bankrup, but the truth of it was we had no choice, it was either going bankrupt or face losing everything we had worked so hard for. It was the morning of hubby's court date and his anxiety was out of control he took double his dose of tablets just to calm the anxiety down, we got to the court at 9 o'clock and went up to sign in, hubby was called in within fifteen minutes he went into see the judge but before he could take a seat the judge turned round to him and said i have granted your bankruptcy so you need to go back down to reception, so we went back down to reception and they told us to come back in an hours time as it would take them that long to sort out the paper work. We left the court and just walked around town until we had to go back, when we got back to the court hubby got his paper work and was told that the official receivers would contact him within the next few days. Hubby was relieved to have it over and done with but still felt so angry that it had come to this all because the system had failed to give us the help we needed, my day at court was yet to come as i was in the next day we still couldn't understand why they couldn't deal with us both at the same time. We went home and just laid on our bed we were still both in disbelief it had come to this. We woke up early the next morning as neither of us got much sleep that night. We had to be at court by 9 o'clock again, it wasn't as quick and easy for me as it was for hubby they kept us hanging around for ages and hubby was due to see a case worker from st clements at 10.30. Whilst we were waiting hubby got a call from the official receivers to discuss his bankruptcy, they didn't speak for long as we had no assets or savings and because the only income we had was my E.S.A they weren't going to close my bank account, they asked to speak to me as we were a couple and they wanted to keep both cases together, i gave them as many details as i could but they said they would ring me the following day as they couldn't proceed anymore until they had received my paperwork. It got to 10 o'clock and i still hadn't been seen so we had to cancel hubbys appointment to see the case worker from st clements. I finally got called in to see the judge at 10.30 and it was just my luck to get a moody judge, he sat me down telling me what i can and can't do but he did grant my bankruptcy, we now had to wait around for another 30 minutes so i could get my paperwork and then that was it all over with we were both now officially bankrupt. Only a few days went by and hubby was in severe pain on his left side also having pain in his lower tummy so we went to the doctors and hubby was sent into hospital he had a load of tests done but the doctor couldn't find what was wrong with him with that after a few hours due to the extent of hubby anxiety being in hospital he discharged himself. More bad luck once again our problems still kept on coming and now for us it was starting to get beyond a joke what was going on with our lifes, none of it made any sense it felt like we were being punished for a crime we didn't commit. How can two people have so much bad luck is beyond my wildest imagination? One thing i am very grateful for is all the problems me and hubby were having along side our depression, anxiety mine and hubby's relationship was still as strong as ever, we had been through so much it would of torn most couples apart but for us it made our relationship even stronger. For me we may have had alot going on but at the end of the day the most important thing was we still had each other. We received a phone call from our daughter on the 1st of June to tell us she was three weeks pregnant, we had mixed emotions as she was struggling for money as it was and personally for me and hubby we felt a little disheartened because we couldn't help our daughter financially like we did with our grandson, so this time the only thing we could do was support her throughout her pregnancy, it took a few days for the news to sink in. Then in the early hours of Saturday 4th of june we got a phone call off of our daughter crying saying mum i am losing blood, so i shot out of bed and took her to A&E. The doctor spoke to our daughter and went through a lot of questions and told her to rest for 48 hours then to return back to the hospital on Monday at 9.45 for a scan. Me and hubby didn't really know what to think why was she bleeding as she had none of this with her little boy, my mind was going back to my sis Lynn and what happened with her pregnancy, my mind was starting to go into over drive all i kept thinking was no more bad luck please. I woke up the following morning in a panic as i had a dream about mum standing at the bottom of my bed with her arms out, i was going towards my mum in my dream thinking she wanted a cuddle from me, then i just saw my mum holding a baby in her arms i found the dream very distressing, as the day went on we received another phone call from our daughter saying that she was bleeding heavier and was passing clots, so me hubby rushed round to our daughters and i ran up into her bedroom and i was shocked to see my daughter standing there looking as white as a ghost. I got on to the phone to the hospital explained what had gone on since Saturday and was told to bring my daughter straight up the hospital were they ran some blood tests, we were told by the doctor that our daughter blood count was at a shocking 7.2 the doctor said he was surprised to still seeing our daughter walking around as anything under 8 is in the danger zone so they kept her in over night to give her fluids and a blood transfusion as she needed 3 pints of blood, i stayed with my daughter over night it was hard because we didn't know if the baby was ok so they done an internal and luckily her cervix was still closed so that was a good sign. We had to wait till the following morning for her to have the scan done to check on the baby it was a hard night but we both got through it, she had her scan and the doctor picked up the babies heartbeat. We were told that everything was fine but they explained that she still could be in the early stages of having a miscarriage but for now the baby was fine. I had my appointment on the same day at 2.45 at the breast clinic so for hubby and i it was all system go again our minds were working overtime, our anxiety was going through the roof everything was all coming at once again, they say bad luck comes in three's but my god ours was coming in bucket loads. My appointment went ok i just had to have some pictures taken of my breasts to help other people that had go through what i did to give them some idea of what the breast can look like when they have had a rebuild, it is helpful because when i was told i had to have a mastectomy i was shown pictures of other women that had already had a rebuild. I was then told to come back up on the 8th which was only in a few days. Life for us was going at a speed of a hundred miles an hour once again, everything was happening all at once with no time to think straight but all the time in the world to worry it just didn't make any sense. The 8th was here before we knew it so i was back up the hospital only to be told that they wanted me to stay under the care of the surgeon that done my operation which meant we had to go out to Bury st Edmunds, i was devastated that i could just be pushed to one side because they weren't willing to take on my aftercare. The doctor that i had was just a stand in and i found him very arrogant, i felt like he just wanted to move on to the next patient. They were not even willing to refer me themselves he just gave me a number and told me to ring them and said that's all. I even had to remind him about my yearly check up that i had to have on my left breast, i was completely shocked by the way i was treated after all what the other surgeon had said on my last appointment there was such lack of communication on their behalf, i found it quite hard to come to terms with if i am completely honest. Once me and hubby had returned home i got straight on to the phone to get my referral sorted and to my amazement he hadn't even give me the right phone number,the numer that i was given turned out to be a pluming service what a joke. After alot of messing about and time wasting i finally got my appointment sorted and within a few weeks i had my letter come through with my appointment booked for the 2nd of September. Our daughter had her 2nd scan as she was still continuing to lose blood, she had her scan and it was good news as the baby was still fine but they had picked up on our daughter having an infection called group b strep which could be the cause of her bleeding, but it also could cause the baby alot of problems through childbirth so this wasn't good news. All this bad luck for no reason and with no answers hubby and i were just going out of our minds with worry. Hubby and i were still having our weekly visits to our doctors and i had the support of my case worker which helped having someone to talk to. Then on the 18th of July i was on the phone talking to my Sis Lynn down stairs in the living room when our daughter had phoned crying to her dad saying to get mum here now dad i have got the baby hanging out of me with that hubby shouted down the stairs to me and said babe we got to go to our daughters nowas she has got the babe hanging out of her, with that i was crying to my sis saying oh no sis what do i do she calmed me down and said go to her, with that me hubby got to our daughters house i ran up the stairs and into her bedroom to find her standing there with blood everywhere i broke down in shock as i kneeled down to have a look to see what was going on and all i could see was this tiny little head no bigger than a ten pence piece just hanging there. There was blood everywhere so we called for an ambulance, once the ambulance got there they took our daughter straight to hospital she was still continuing to pass blood and she was in so much pain. We had to wait for the doctor to come and see her as he was caught up in theatre so the nurses were just changing the sheets over and over because she was losing so much blood, finally the doctor came in he asked a few questions then said he wanted to do an internal to see what was going on. Whilst she was having her internal done she was holding on to my hand so tight, the doctor told her to cough and then push down into her bum, i knew then that she had lost her babe but i wasn't going to believe it until we knew for sure. Once the procedure was over with the doctor walked out, he came back in a few minutes later and said i am so sorry to have to tell you this but you have just lost your baby. We were all so distraught and heartbroken my poor daughter she never said a word, i took her to the bathroom and she just broke down crying saying mum i have lost my baby, i was trying to be so strong for her but i just couldn't so i broke down to. We were just in complete shock emotionally and physically i can't find any words in my heart to explain how we all felt, we knew that there was a strong chance she could lose the babe but for once we were just hoping luck would be on our side this time. Me and hubby left the hospital in early hours of the morning and just before i left i looked at my daughter with tears in my eyes and said darling your baby is going to be fine, he or she is going to be with their great nanny now, she never got to meet any of her grand children but she has got to meet her great great grandchild now and mum will take care of your baby you can bank on that my darling, she replied with tears in her eyes i know mum. It was so hard to just walk out of the hospital that night being her mum i just wanted to hold her in my arms but our daughter needed to be with her partner, as me hubby walked out of the hospital making our way back to our car i could finally let out how i felt. My emotions were not going to hold back for nothing it was as if someone had just turned on a tap, i was crying all the way home hubby was just in limbo, we got home at three in the morning i was still in tears i had so many mixed emotions and i was so angry, i kept saying why what more are you going to do to us haven't we suffered enough, i just couldn't get my daughter out of my mind. Early the following morning me and hubby left to go to our daughters house to get our grandson as our youngest son was looking after him, i had to go into her bedroom and clean up her room ready for when she got home, i didn't want her to come home to what i had to see as there was blood everywhere on the floor, the pillows and a towel still in the same place where our daughter had been laying it just broke my heart. As i was on the floor cleaning all the blood up my grandson walked into the bedroom and sat next to me and pointed to the spots of blood on the floor and said mummy, he kept trying to help me clean it up, again i felt as if someone had ripped my heart out, i just wanted my grandson out of the room i didn't want him to see that, but he wanted to be with his nanny and help clean up. Once we had cleaned the house we left and took our grandson back home to be with us as our daughter had to stay in until later on in the day, hubby played with our grandson trying to take his mind off of things as all he kept on saying was mummy. We kept in touch with our daughter throughout the day by phone so she could keep us updated to what was going on, she told us she was waiting for her blood test results then she would be coming home so with that i started to get ready to go pick them up from the hospital. I got the call about half an hour later from our daughter saying mum can you come get us please, i got the babe ready and left to pick my daughter up all she wanted to do was hold her son but he had fallen asleep on our way up to the hospital. So with that my daughter got in the front seat of the car with me and my heart went out to her, we spoke about her baby and she was very emotional, it was hard for us all especially for my daughter as she carried her babe for 11 short weeks. I can't say i understand what she was going through as i had never experienced a miscarrage myself so i didn't know how she would of been feeling, all i know is in my own heart she must of been feeling so empty knowing that she had her baby inside of her and now there was nothing. Once we got to her home i went in with her to make sure she was ok and stayed with her for a while, i knew i had to let her be by herself with her son. For me and hubby having to watch our daughter lose her baby is one of most devastating experiences we will ever go through, instead of a happy ending she was so looking forward to, we all as a family had to deal with shock and disbelief of our daughter losing her baby. It makes me realise your not in control of your life and we believe we can control our destiny if we try hard enough, but sometimes fate takes that control away from us. As the last page in my book was still already full of pain and heartache a brand new page for me unfolds. God broke our hearts once again to prove to us he still only takes the best even though our daughter only made it through her pregnancy to 11 short weeks it was still a baby, it was still a life, so quickly you came into our lifes then so quickly torn away we never got the chance to meet you, where there was once joy and happiness, there is now sadness and pain sleep on our unknown child we will never forget you R.I.P baby lette'. For me and hubby things are still the same depression still plays a big part in our lifes and we don't know what life has in store for us. I still know i have to face one more operation if i choose to" who knows". We all make decisions in our lifes that we have to live with good and bad, but the one thing i have always missed in my life is having my mum to turn to for advice as we had a relationship that could never be replaced, i have a loving husband that would give me the world if he could, three loving children that are my world and a gorgeous grandson, but my life still feels incomplete. Ever since i lost my mum it has felt like i have a hole in my heart that just can't be filled no matter how hard i try. I think that is why i have always wanted to write this book because my mum was someone so special to me and i have always tried to keep the memory of my mum alive.

THIS BOOK IS IN THE LOVING MEMORY OF MY MUM AND THE
AMAZING LEGACY SHE HAD LEFT BEHIND
ACKNOWLEDGMENTS
I just wanted to thank those who where there for me throughout
my ordeal with the radial scar.
I want to thank my sis Lynn who has been there for me through
the past 2 years
Thanks to my auntie and her family for their support since the loss
of my nana and being there for me emotionally
I'd like to thank our three children for trying their best to help
and their patience
And finally a huge thank you to my husband Steve for all the love
and support even though he was suffering himself as i could
not of done this without him

IN LOVING MEMORY OF ALL THOSE THAT I HAVE
LOVED AND LOST
THE FOLLOWING POEM IS DEDICATED TO MY MUM

DEEP WITHIN THE HEART OF ME
HIDDEN WHERE NO ONE CAN SEE
IS A BOOK MORE PRECIOUS THAN GOLD
WHERE THE STORY OF LIFE WITHOUT MUM UNFOLDS
22 YEARS SINCE WE SAID GOODBYE
BUT MY LOVE FOR YOU WILL NEVER DIE
A THOUSAND WORDS WILL NEVER SAY
HOW MUCH I MISS YOU STILL TODAY
A LOVING SMILE, A HEART OF GOLD
NO DEARER MOTHER THIS WORLD COULD HOLD
THE PAIN INSIDE GOES ON AND ON
AND WILL UNTIL MY LIFE HAS GONE
THE HARDEST THING IN LIFE TO BAIR
IS TO WANT MY MUM BUT SHE'S NOT THERE
I KNOW WE ARE NOT SIDE BY SIDE I KNOW WE ARE APART
BUT NO MATTER WHERE I GO I'LL ALWAYS HAVE YOUR HEART.